Kimberly Akimbo

ALSO BY DAVID LINDSAY-ABAIRE

Fuddy Meers
Wonder of the World

Kimberly Akimbo

David Lindsay-Abaire

THE OVERLOOK PRESS
WOODSTOCK & NEW YORK

CAUTION: Professionals and amateurs are hereby warned that performance of KIMBERLY AKIMBO is subject to a royalty. It is fully protected under the copyright laws of the United States of America, and of all countries covered by the International Copyright Union (including the Dominion of Canada and the rest of the British Commonwealth), and of all countries covered by the Pan-American Copyright Convention, the Universal Copyright Convention, the Berne Convention, and of all countries with which the United States has reciprocal copyright relations. All rights, including professional/amateur stage rights, motion picture, recitation, lecturing, public reading, radio broadcasting, television, video or sound recording, all other forms of mechanical or electronic reproduction, such as CD-ROM, CD-I, DVD, information storage and retrieval systems and photocopying, and the rights of translation into foreign languages, are strictly reserved. Particular emphasis is placed upon the matter of readings, permission for which must be secured from the Author's agent in writing.

The stage performance rights in KIMBERLY AKIMBO (other than first class rights) are controlled exclusively by DRAMATISTS PLAY SERVICE, INC., 440 Park Avenue South, New York, NY 10016. No professional or non-professional performance of the Play (excluding first class professional performance) may be given without obtaining in advance the written permission of DRAMATISTS PLAY SERVICE, INC., and paying the requisite fee.

Inquiries concerning all other rights should be addressed to The Gersh Agency, 41 Madison Avenue, 33rd floor, New York, NY 10036. Attn: John Buzzetti.

First published in the United States in 2004 by
The Overlook Press, Peter Mayer Publishers, Inc.
Woodstock & New York

WOODSTOCK:
One Overlook Drive
Woodstock, NY 12498
www.overlookpress.com
[for individual orders, bulk and special sales, contact our Woodstock office]

NEW YORK:
141 Wooster Street
New York, NY 10012

Copyright © 1999, 2003 by David Lindsay-Abaire

All Rights Reserved. No part of this publication may be reproduced or transmitted in any form or by any means, electronic or mechanical, including photocopy, recording, or any information storage and retrieval system now known or to be invented without permission in writing from the publisher, except by a reviewer who wishes to quote brief passages in connection with a review written for inclusion in a magazine, newspaper, or broadcast.

Cataloging-in-Publication Data is available from the Library of Congress.

Book design and type formatting by Bernard Schleifer
Manufactured in the United States of America
FIRST EDITION
1 3 5 7 9 8 6 4 2
ISBN 1-58567-480-X (pb)

Introduction

> How true Daddy's words were when he said: "All children must look after their own upbringing." Parents can only give good advice or put them on the right paths, but the final forming of a person's character lies in their own hands.
>
> —Anne Frank (1929–45), *The Diary of a Young Girl*

> LORD ILLINGWORTH: The soul is born old and grows young. That is the comedy of life.
>
> MRS. ALLONBY: And the body is born young and grows old. That is life's tragedy.
>
> —Oscar Wilde (1854–1900), *A Woman of No Importance*

So, it's time to write another introduction. Honestly, I never enjoy this. I'm thrilled that someone is actually willing to publish another play of mine, but I always find the task of writing an intro terribly daunting. I scanned my bookshelf to see if I could get inspiration from other playwrights, but most of their introductions were written by *other* people. Which gave me pause. If Tony Kushner didn't have to write an introduction, why did *I*? Yes, I know *he's* won a Pulitzer and I haven't, but so what?

And then it occurred to me that maybe my publishers *did* in fact try to find someone to write my introduction but no one was willing to do it, which of course started to make me a little sad. But then I took a few Vicodin, and now I feel *much* better. I'm kidding. I don't take pills. I have a delicate stomach.

But if I *could* choose someone to write an introduction to my play, it would have to be Katie Couric. I don't believe she's actually familiar with my work, but she seems like a very nice lady, doesn't she? Smart and yet approachable. I like that in a person. If I weren't married, I'd probably ask Katie Couric on a date. Yes, she's a little older than I am, but that's very hip nowadays, I'm told. I think Katie and I would make a lovely couple.

I seem to be rambling. This is why I shouldn't write my own introductions. I suppose there may be a segue in there somewhere, though. Let's see . . . Me and Katie Couric. May-December romances. *Kimberly Akimbo.* Ah yes, here we go, the romance in *Kimberly* is between two teenagers, but one *looks* like an old lady, so . . . Not that, Katie Couric looks like an old lady. In fact, I think she looks *great,* and I'm pretty sure that she hasn't had any work done, which I understand is very rare with celebrities. Do you think Robert Redford had his eyes done? I heard that once. Not sure if it's true, though. If I was Katie Couric, and I was interviewing Robert Redford, that would be my first question. "Mr. Redford, is it true you've had plastic surgery performed on your eyes?" And if I were Robert Redford, I might be offended by that question, but then I'd let it go, because, really, how could you stay mad at Katie Couric? I think Robert Redford and Katie Couric would also make a lovely couple, even though he's much older than she is, which brings us right back to the topic of *Kimberly Akimbo.*

I've recently mentioned to a few people that this introduction was due, and the response was usually "Oh, are you going to write one of those funny little scenes, like you did for the intros to *Fuddy Meers* and *Wonder of the World?* Those are my *favorite* parts of your plays!" Which seems like an odd thing to say, doesn't it? I mean, I slave over a play for a couple years, finally get it produced and published, and their FAVORITE part is a three-page scene in my intro that I whipped off overnight? Maybe I'm just sensitive.

Anyway, since I couldn't get anyone to write my introduction *for* me, I thought I'd at least get someone to talk with me about my work, but everyone I asked seemed too shy (or at least that's how I chose to interpret their deafeningly silent responses). Well, since a big part of the play is about the relationship between parents and their children, I thought it might be interesting to talk to my own son about the play. It went like this . . .

(David Lindsay-Abaire's living room. He sits with a stack of neatly typed index cards ala James Lipton on Inside the Actors Studio. David's son, Nicholas, sits in a chair across from him. Nicholas is two years old.)

DAVID LINDSAY-ABAIRE
Hello, Nicholas.

NICHOLAS
Hi, Da-da.

INTRODUCTION

DAVID LINDSAY-ABAIRE
I'd like to first thank you for sitting down with me and agreeing to discuss my work.

NICHOLAS
Hi, Da-da.

DAVID LINDSAY-ABAIRE
We already said hello.

NICHOLAS
Big hug?

DAVID LINDSAY-ABAIRE
Sure . . .
(*leans over and hugs Nicholas*)

NICHOLAS
Danks.

DAVID LINDSAY-ABAIRE
You're welcome.

NICHOLAS
I wanna cashew.

DAVID LINDSAY-ABAIRE
We're not eating cashews right now; we're talking about Daddy's play.

NICHOLAS
Carry me?

DAVID LINDSAY-ABAIRE
Uhh, all right. Hop up.

(*Nicholas climbs out of his chair and onto his dad's lap. David flips over an index card.*)

DAVID LINDSAY-ABAIRE
My first question is about the tone in my work. How would you characterize it?

NICHOLAS
Hmm.

DAVID LINDSAY-ABAIRE
Take your time.

NICHOLAS
(*after long pause*)
Da blue fish was funny. In da movies wit da puck-corn. And a booster seat. For you too? NO! Ony Nicholas. You too big. Memba dat?

DAVID LINDSAY-ABAIRE
I do, but I'm gonna need you to focus a little, okay?

NICHOLAS
And Nemo's Daddy went sssssooom and da sharks. You da Daddy. Like Nemo's Daddy. But you wear shoes.

DAVID LINDSAY-ABAIRE
That's true.

NICHOLAS
I wear shoes too.

DAVID LINDSAY-ABAIRE
Okay, let's try another question.
(*flips over another index card*)
Who's your favorite character in *Kimberly Akimbo*, and could you provide an amusing anecdote to help illustrate that choice?

NICHOLAS
I wanna cashew.

DAVID LINDSAY-ABAIRE
Nicholas, we talked about the cashews already.

NICHOLAS
I want one.

DAVID LINDSAY-ABAIRE
We don't have any more.

NICHOLAS
I wanna cashew.

DAVID LINDSAY-ABAIRE
The cashews are gone.

NICHOLAS
Dey take da F Train?

DAVID LINDSAY-ABAIRE
No, they didn't take the F Train. We ate them.

NICHOLAS
In da belly?

DAVID LINDSAY-ABAIRE
That's right.
(*Nicholas considers this for a long time.*)

NICHOLAS
I want one dough.

DAVID LINDSAY-ABAIRE
I know. Isn't life hard?
(*Nicholas just stares at him blankly.*)
Can we go back to Daddy's index cards?

NICHOLAS
No. I big now, and you da baby.
(*scrambles off his dad's lap*)

DAVID LINDSAY-ABAIRE
Nicholas—

NICHOLAS
No Nicholas. I da *Daddy*. Dose are mine.
(*Nicholas grabs the index cards and begins running around the room with them.*)

DAVID LINDSAY-ABAIRE
Nicholas, you need to stop running.

NICHOLAS
NO! *You* stop! You da baby! I da Daddy!

DAVID LINDSAY-ABAIRE
You give me my index cards *right* now.

NICHOLAS
My cards!
(*yells*)
MINE! I DA DADDY!

DAVID LINDSAY-ABAIRE
That is an *outdoor* voice. What'd we say about out—

NICHOLAS
Time for you to go to sleep. I get your blanket.
(*runs off into another room*)

DAVID LINDSAY-ABAIRE
I don't *want* a blanket. You get back here. Nicholas?
(*no response*)
Nicholas, I need those cards. If you don't want to do this interview, I'll call up your Nana instead. Maybe she'll answer some questions.
(*long pause*)
Nicholas?

(*A toilet flushes in another room.*)

DAVID LINDSAY-ABAIRE
What are you doing? You're not toilet-trained yet.
(*Nicholas comes back in with a little blanket.*)

NICHOLAS
Here's da blanket. Time for da baby to go to sleep.
(*holds out the blanket to David*)

DAVID LINDSAY-ABAIRE
Where are my index cards?

NICHOLAS
Dey all gone. Dey with da cashews maybe.

DAVID LINDSAY-ABAIRE
Nicholas, I worked very hard on those questions.

NICHOLAS
Dey went down down down.

DAVID LINDSAY-ABAIRE
Did you flush my index cards?

NICHOLAS
Shh, go to sleep, baby.

DAVID LINDSAY-ABAIRE
But I needed them. For the interview.

NICHOLAS

I know. Isn't life hard?

(*Nicholas tucks the blanket around his dad.
End of interview.*)

This little "scene" will make a lot more sense after you've read the play, I promise. Inversion of parent-child roles and whatnot. You'll see.

Now that I have a child, a lot of people ask if *Kimberly* came out of my experiences as a Dad, which is sort of a horrifying question if you know the play at all. *Kimberly* was actually finished right before Nicholas was born. "So where did it come from?" they always ask. Usually I say Taiwan. Which makes absolutely no sense. Unless you know me. Which few people really do, I'd say. The *real* me, I mean. The me who sips tequila in the wee hours and longs to play banjo. But I digress. Okay, where did *Kimberly Akimbo* come from? One would assume that my experiences with my own parents must be a huge part of the play, but since they may be reading this intro I wholeheartedly refute that assumption (wink wink).

In truth, the seed of the play came when I asked a friend how his new niece was. He said, "Oh, she's amazing! So wise! She's two months going on eighty years old!" And because I'm such a literal-minded person, I immediately pictured a tiny old woman trapped in the body of an infant, which is, I suppose, kind of funny but also kind of disturbing, which is how most people describe my plays, so that seemed like a good place to start. Then I remembered a documentary I had seen a long time ago about progeria, which is a disease that causes premature aging in children. And I certainly knew that that specific condition was far too sad and complicated for me to put into a comedy, but I couldn't let go of the idea of a child wise beyond her years contending with the everyday challenges of growing up while simultaneously dealing with the physical challenges of growing old. And since I had no interest in writing a medical drama, I felt free to fictionalize the disease significantly in order to tell the story I wanted to tell: a girl desperately trying to live a normal life despite the ever-present specter of her own mortality.

I also knew that an older actress would play the teenage girl, and about halfway through writing the first act, I started to hear the voice of Marylouise Burke reciting Kimberly's lines. Marylouise is a wonderfully spirited, hilarious, and profoundly truthful actress who had appeared in three of my previous plays, including *Fuddy Meers*, in which she played an aphasic stroke victim who spoke gibberish for the entire show. Once I had Marylouise inside my head (she must've been terrified), the play pretty much took off and wrote itself.

I say it wrote itself, but really, I had a lot of help, starting first and foremost with South Coast Rep, which commissioned the play and produced its world premiere. I owe a tremendous amount to Jerry Patch, David Emmes, Martin Benson, Paula Tomei, Mark Rucker, Joanne DeNaut, Nancy Levy, the entire SCR staff, and the uber-talented Joanna Adler, Ann Dowd, and Steven Flynn, who all helped bring this play to life.

For the New York premiere, I was thrilled to be working yet again at Manhattan Theatre Club, which has been my theatrical home since they premiered *Fuddy Meers* in 1999. Lynne Meadow, Barry Grove, and the sainted MTC staff (especially David Caparelliotis, Paige Evans, and Nancy Piccione) gave us an ideal and idyllic environment to work in. Happily, the entire South Coast Rep design team was reassembled to work their magic in New York. Huge thanks to Robert Brill, Marty Pakledinaz, Bruce Ellman, Jason Robert Brown, and Brian MacDevitt (even if he did rag on the Red Sox incessantly.) Even bigger thanks to my inspired and inspiring director, David Petrarca, and my unmatchable cast: Ana Gasteyer, Jake Weber, Jodie Markell, the unflappable John Gallagher, Jr. (who had been with the play since that sweltering summer at the O'Neill), and, caught somewhere between Melpomene and Thalia, the singular muse that is Marylouise Burke.

In addition, I got tremendous support from Seth Gordon, Casey Childs, and the Primary Stages New American Writers Group, as well as James Houghton and everyone at the Eugene O'Neill National Playwrights Conference. Thanks also to Jessica Bauman, Joy Carlin, Ramona Collier, Cusi Cram, Murphy Davis, Jason Scott Eagan, Edie Falco, Melissa Gallagher, Madeleine George, Daniel Goldfarb, Rinne Groff, Jan Leslie Harding, O. Aldon James Jr. and the National Arts Club, Julia Jordan, Joe Kraemer, Deb Laufer, Antoinette Lavecchia, John Bedford Lloyd, Kate Loewald, Mike Lubin, Danny Mastrogiorgio, Ryan McMahon, Michael Moody, Didi O'Connell, Michael O'Conner, Michael Parva, Jim Pentecost, Patti Perkins, David Pressman, Ilana Rose, Gareth Saxe, Julian Sheppard, Debra Waxman, my crossword partner Max Wilk, Daniel Zaitchik, my stalwart shepherd John Buzzetti, and, as always, my midwife in everything, Chris Lindsay-Abaire, who holds my hand, wipes my brow, reminds me to breathe, and tells me to push.

And with that lovely image, I sign off.

DAVID LINDSAY-ABAIRE
August, 2003

Kimberly Akimbo

KIMBERLY AKIMBO was commissioned, developed, and first produced by South Coast Repertory (David Emmes, Producing Artistic Director; Martin Benson, Artistic Director) in Costa Mesa, CA, premiering on May 13, 2001. It was directed by David Petrarca; the set design was by Robert Brill; the lighting design was by Brian MacDevitt; the costume design was by Martin Pakledinaz; the sound design was by Bruce Ellman; the original music was composed by Jason Robert Brown; the dramaturg was Jerry Patch; the Production Manager was Tom Aberger; and the Stage Manager was Randall K. Lum. The cast was as follows:

Kimberly	Marylouise Burke
Buddy	Steven Flynn
Jeff	John Gallagher, Jr.
Pattie	Ann Dowd
Debra	Joanna P. Adler

A revised version of KIMBERLY AKIMBO was produced by Manhattan Theatre Club (Lynne Meadow, Artistic Director; Barry Grove, Executive Producer) in New York City on January 14, 2003. It was directed by David Petrarca; the set design was by Robert Brill; the lighting design was by Brian MacDevitt; the costume design was by Martin Pakledinaz; the sound design was by Bruce Ellman; the original music was composed by Jason Robert Brown; and the Production Stage Manager was Jason Scott Eagan. The cast was as follows:

Kimberly	Marylouise Burke
Buddy	Jake Weber
Jeff	John Gallagher, Jr.
Pattie	Jodie Markell
Debra	Ana Gasteyer

Time

the present

Place

Bogota, New Jersey
(pronounced buh-GO-da)

Cast

Kimberly—a 16-year-old-girl, played by a woman in her 60's or 70's

Buddy—a man in his mid-30's, Kimberly's dad

Pattie—a very pregnant woman in her mid-30's, Buddy's wife

Jeff—an awkward, unpopular 16-year-old boy

Debra—a woman in her early 30's, an ex-con, Pattie's sister

Set

The set, with its multiple locations, should be simple and somewhat representational. Nothing should stop the flow of the play.

Act One

Scene One

(A blast of cold wind, sounds of winter, wind howling, maybe snow on a scrim.

Lights come up on a bench outside. An old woman sits, shivering. She looks at her watch. She wears a hooded parka and boots. She has ice skates, tied at the laces, slung over her shoulder. KIMBERLY *is 16, but she's played by an actress in her 60's or 70's. She looks at her watch again.*

Far upstage, buddy, *mid-30's, runs through the snow like a kid. He spots* KIM.*)*

BUDDY

Hey, Kimmy! How crazy is this?!
    (jogs down to the bench)
Can you believe it's April?! It's like a Christmas card out here! It's pretty though, right?! Maybe tomorrow'll be a snow-day! Look at it coming down! You didn't wanna wait inside?

KIMBERLY

It closed at eight.

BUDDY

The rink closed?
    (looks at watch)
What time is it?

KIMBERLY

Ten-thirty.

BUDDY
Really?
(looks at watch, taps it)

KIMBERLY
I can't feel my feet.

BUDDY
I told you to wear extra socks.

KIMBERLY
Where were you?

BUDDY
I got caught up. I'm sorry.

KIMBERLY
You suck.

BUDDY
Hey, don't be like that. You wanna make a snow angel?

KIMBERLY
You said you'd pick me up at eight and you didn't and that sucks.

BUDDY
Now come on. You've got gloves.

KIMBERLY
Two and a half hours. It's like four degrees out here. I could've died.

BUDDY
Howya gonna die with that big fluffy parka?

KIMBERLY
The zipper's busted.

BUDDY
I had some trouble with the car.

KIMBERLY
Yeah, right.

BUDDY
You couldn't get a ride with someone else?

KIMBERLY
You said you'd pick me up.

BUDDY
Did you eat?

KIMBERLY
You said we'd get drive-through.

BUDDY
You must be hungry.

KIMBERLY
Oh, you think *maybe*? You suck.

BUDDY
Why didn't you call Pattie?

KIMBERLY
The buttons on the pay phone are frozen.

BUDDY
You should've breathed on them. Heated them up.

KIMBERLY
She can't answer the phone anyway.

BUDDY
Right.

KIMBERLY
Her bandages are too big.

BUDDY
I know. I'm sorry.

KIMBERLY
Everybody else got picked up.

BUDDY
You're not getting any warmer sitting there.

KIMBERLY
Well, I'd love to move, but my ass is frozen to the bench.

BUDDY
Let's go, we'll drive by the Zippy Burger.

KIMBERLY
I don't want to.

BUDDY
Come on, Kimberly. You gonna be difficult now?

KIMBERLY
I don't know. You gonna be concerned now?

BUDDY
Fine, you wanna sit, we'll sit.
   (he sits)
How was ice skating?

KIMBERLY
Are you okay to drive?
   (no response)
Dad?
   (no response)
Are you okay to drive?

BUDDY
Yes.

KIMBERLY
Because I know where you were.

BUDDY
If your mom asks, we'll explain about the car trouble.

   (The lights change.)

Scene Two

(The bench turns into a car. BUDDY *is driving.)*

BUDDY
Do me a favor and play it cool. Don't make trouble with your mother. She's very anxious about the baby.

KIMBERLY
Uh-huh.

BUDDY
She says it's kicking too much. I explained that's what babies do, but you know your mother. I remember you kicked a lot too.

KIMBERLY
Maybe that's what she's anxious about.

BUDDY
No, that has nothing to do with— She's still adjusting. Getting used to Bogota.

KIMBERLY
Whatever.

BUDDY
Just don't rile her up, 'cause she'll take it out on me.
(*The car pulls into a Zippy Burger drive-thru.* BUDDY *rolls down his window.*)

JEFF
(*over speaker*)
Welcome to Zippy Burger. My name is Jeff. Can I take your order?

BUDDY
Two Cheezy Burgers, two Frenchy Fries, and one large Coke.
(*to* KIMBERLY)
It's okay if we share the soda?

KIMBERLY
Fine.

JEFF
(*over the speaker*)
Anything else, sir?

BUDDY
No. That's it.
(*to* KIMBERLY)
You look a little better. Color's coming back into your face. You feel thawed out?

JEFF
(*over the speaker*)
Is that Kimberly Levaco?
(BUDDY *looks from the speaker to* KIMBERLY.)

JEFF
(*over speaker*)
I can see you in the camera. Is that Kimberly Levaco?

BUDDY
Who wants to know?

JEFF
(*over speaker*)
Jeff.

BUDDY
(*to* KIMBERLY)
Do you know a Jeff?

JEFF
(*over speaker*)
Jeff McCracken.

BUDDY
Do you know a Jeff McCracken?

JEFF
(*over speaker*)
I'm in her biology class. Are you her father?

BUDDY
Yes I am. Can I help you?

JEFF
(*over speaker*)
I have a question to ask her.

BUDDY
(*to* KIMBERLY)
What's this numb-nuts want?

JEFF
(*over speaker*)
I can still hear you, sir.

KIMBERLY
I don't know.

JEFF
(*over speaker*)
I just want to ask her something.

BUDDY
Sounds like a jack-ass.

JEFF
(*over speaker*)
Still listening, sir.

BUDDY
Get my Cheezy Burgers.

JEFF
(*over speaker*)
You can pull around and pay at the window. I'll see you there.

(BUDDY *pulls around.*)

BUDDY
I'll tell you what. If you don't upset your mom tonight, I'll take you to Six Flags Great Adventure.

KIMBERLY
Dad, you've been saying that since forever, and we've never gone, so give it up. 'Cause it's a lame-ass bribe.

(JEFF *appears at the drive-thru window in a Zippy Burger uniform. He's 16, not the most popular kid.*)

JEFF
Hi.

BUDDY
Hello.

JEFF
That'll be five sixty-three, please. Hi, Kimberly.

KIMBERLY
Hi.

BUDDY
Do you take food stamps?

KIMBERLY

Dad—

BUDDY

What?

JEFF

I'm sorry, sir, we don't.

BUDDY

(*to* KIMBERLY)
I was kidding.
(*to* JEFF)
Gimme a second.
(*gets money together*)

KIMBERLY

What were you gonna ask me?

JEFF

It's about that bio assignment.

KIMBERLY

What about it?

JEFF

You know how we have to write a paper about a disease?

KIMBERLY

Yeah.

JEFF

Well, I wanted to know if I could talk to you. About yours. Your disease. You know, how you look old and everything but really you're not.

BUDDY

(*pays him*)
Here, that's exact change. Gimme the food.

JEFF

Because I thought not too many people would pick that one. Could I talk to you about it?

BUDDY

Kimberly's busy this week. Pick another disease.

JEFF
(*hands food to* BUDDY)
Oh. Because, I thought I could just talk to her about it. It wouldn't take long—

BUDDY
Thanks, but no. Have a good night now.
(BUDDY *peels away.* JEFF *disappears.*)

BUDDY
That kid's a weirdo. I don't like him. We'll go to the B.K. next time.
(*looks over at her*)
Sorry about that, honey.

KIMBERLY
I don't care.

BUDDY
What are *you* gonna write about?

KIMBERLY
Glaucoma.

BUDDY
Oh, that's a good one.

KIMBERLY
I guess.

BUDDY
Hey, you know what else? They have a Safari at Six Flags now. A big one. You drive through and all these wild animals shit on your car. Giraffes and gorillas. All right here in New Jersey. You wanna do that?

KIMBERLY
Sure.

BUDDY
(*pause*)
That boy wasn't being very sensitive.

KIMBERLY
I said I didn't care.

                          BUDDY
Okay.
   (pause)
I almost thought he was gonna ask you out.
   (Lights crossfade to . . .)

Scene Three

(*Lights up on a tape recorder on a kitchen table.* pattie, *in her mid-30's, sits at the table. She wears a house-coat and slippers and is very pregnant. Her hands are wrapped in bandages. Except for the light over the table, the kitchen is dark. It's late.* PATTIE *looks at the tape recorder.*)

                          PATTIE
Okay, here we go. Let's see. Record.
   (*She tries to press record, but her bandages are too big. She tries again.*)

                          PATTIE
Jesus. How am I supposed to—?
   (*She tries with her elbow, her knee, her head, her nose, etc.*)

                          PATTIE
   (*trying with her chin*)
Ow— I can't— Stupid piece of crap—
   (*click*)
   (PATTIE *sits up in disbelief. It's recording. She's winded but pleasantly surprised. She leans over and speaks into the recorder sweetly.*)

                          PATTIE
Hello, darling. This is your mother speaking. You're in my belly right now. And sometimes you kick me. Isn't that precious? Now listen to me, sweetheart, because people are going to tell you awful things about me. You mustn't believe them. People lie. They are hateful cock-suckers. All of them. People spread vicious lies when their victims aren't around to defend themselves. Remember that when I'm dead and someone tells you I was a demonic bitch. You stand up and tell them that I was sweet and funny and you have the tapes to prove it. It's always

good to have evidence, sweetheart. That's why I'm making you this tape. I wanna make sure you get your info from the horse's mouth, because I'm gonna drop dead any second.
(*beat*)
On the bright side, I just got my Carpal Tunnel operation, so I may be able to use my hands before I die. We'll see. All those years in Secaucus took their toll. Sixteen years I worked in the Sunshine Cupcake Factory, pumping cream into those Ding-Dong knock-offs. Sixteen years of squeezing that goddam cream gun. That's one of the reasons we moved away from Secaucus. Not the *main* reason, but one of them.
(*beat*)
I hope I get to breast-feed. That's my one wish. If I give birth to you and they let me breast-feed, then I can die happily. I didn't get to do that with your sister. She was so bad off when she came out that they took her straight to I.C.U. They say that mother-child bond is so important, and it starts that very first moment. But she was never placed on my chest, and I never cooed over her, and she was never breast-fed, so I think we never had that. The bond thing.

(*A door slams.* BUDDY *and* KIMBERLY *enter.* BUDDY *clicks on the kitchen lights and hangs the car keys on a little hook on the wall of the kitchen.* KIM *sets up to start her homework at the table.*)

PATTIE
Where the hell were you?

BUDDY
Car problems. We had to get a jump.

PATTIE
I'm starving. You bring me a Zippy Fish?

BUDDY
Did you want one?

PATTIE
Son of a bitch.

BUDDY
I'm sorry.

PATTIE
I've gotta eat, Buddy! I'm pregnant!

BUDDY
I know.

PATTIE
Kim's in charge of my meals from now on. Okay, Kim?

KIMBERLY
Whatever.

PATTIE
I'll starve if I have to rely on your father one more day.

KIMBERLY
What's with the tape recorder?

PATTIE
I'm creating an oral history for the baby. This kid's gonnna know me better than any of you.
(*beat*)
Now tell the truth, Kim. Why were you late?

KIMBERLY
(*pause*)
The battery died. We had to get a jump.

PATTIE
From who?

KIMBERLY
Just a guy in a truck.

PATTIE
What kind of truck?

KIMBERLY
A . . . chicken truck.

PATTIE
A chicken truck?

KIMBERLY
Yeah. It was filled with chickens.

PATTIE

I *know* what a chicken truck is. Kinda cold to be transporting poultry, isn't it?

KIMBERLY

I don't know.

PATTIE

Huh. Maybe a chicken truck'll pull over for *me* some day. Maybe chicken-guy will give me a jump when *I* die.

BUDDY

You're not gonna die, Pattie. We were just a little late.

PATTIE

You smell like gasoline.

BUDDY

I work at a gas-station, honey.

PATTIE

Do you also work in a bar-room? Because I smell a little bit of that too.

BUDDY

Pattie—

KIMBERLY

Maybe we could have a real dinner tomorrow.
(*They look at her as if she's speaking Greek.*)
Instead of take-out. A sit-down dinner.

PATTIE

Is that a dig?

KIMBERLY

No.

PATTIE

You know I can't cook meals in this condition.

KIMBERLY

Dad can do it. After work. He'll cook something healthy. It'll be good for the baby.

PATTIE

Oh. Well, that's all right then. It's a nice idea, isn't it, Bud?

BUDDY

(*beat*)
Sure. I could do that.

KIMBERLY

A roast maybe. Vegetables. Some cake for dessert.

BUDDY

I'll decide what to cook. Don't push it, Kim.

PATTIE

Did I mention I met one of the neighbors today?

BUDDY

(*suddenly on edge*)
No, what neighbor?

PATTIE

Relax, Buddy. They're nice people. You need to work on your social skills.
(*to* KIMBERLY)
He's so suspicious about neighbors.

BUDDY

Yeah, I wonder why?

PATTIE

You leave me alone for hours, I'm gonna talk to people. I need to do *something* to occupy my time! For fucksake, Buddy . . .

KIMBERLY

Do you guys wanna try an experiment?

BUDDY

What?

PATTIE

Oo, she's a mad scientist.

BUDDY

What experiment? For school?

KIMBERLY

No, just for fun. I had an idea.
(*goes to a cabinet*)

BUDDY
You're full of ideas tonight, aren't ya?
(KIM *takes an empty jar from the cabinet and places it in the middle of the table.*)

PATTIE
(*beat*)
I hope you don't expect me to piss in that.

KIMBERLY
This family swears too much.

PATTIE
Says who? I don't swear.

KIMBERLY
You just said piss and fucksake.

PATTIE
Hey! Watch your mouth!

KIMBERLY
I propose that every time one of us swears, we have to put a nickel in the jar as a punishment.

BUDDY
Like a challenge. That's good. I love a challenge.

PATTIE
Yeah *right*. You love to *run away* from a challenge, you mean.
(*turns to* KIM *and chuckles*)
Ya hear that? He loves a challenge.

BUDDY
I married you, didn't I?

PATTIE
You coulda done a lot worse than me. Hell, I'm no challenge. I'm a straightforward, easy ride. I'm the Kansas of wives.

KIMBERLY
So yes to the jar?

PATTIE
Who gets the money when we're done?

KIMBERLY

The baby. We'll buy a Jolly Jumper.

PATTIE

Well that sounds fair.

KIMBERLY

Dad?

BUDDY

Okay.

KIMBERLY

All right then. Let's start . . . *now*.
    (*The three of them stare at the jar in silence. After a pause . . .*)

BUDDY

I don't understand what we're supposed to do.

KIMBERLY

Nothing. Just . . . do whatever, but don't swear while you do it.

BUDDY

Oh.
    (KIMBERLY *goes back to her homework.*)

BUDDY

So what neighbor did you meet?

PATTIE

Mrs. Gigante.

BUDDY

How'd you meet her?

PATTIE

I called to her from the window. I said "Howdy, neighbor. What's your name?"

BUDDY

What'd she say?

PATTIE

She said, "Mrs. Gigante." Whaddaya think she said? Do you even listen to me?

(turns to KIM*)*
Is it *me*? Am *I* the crazy one?

KIMBERLY
Honestly, it's a flip of the coin.

PATTIE
What?

KIMBERLY
Nothing.

PATTIE
Don't mumble, Kimmy. I may be going deaf.

BUDDY
Lucky you.

PATTIE
Mrs. Gigante's daughter, Bonnie, is in a dance recital on Sunday.

BUDDY
The blonde girl? Isn't she in your class, Kim?

PATTIE
She takes lessons at the Miss Maxie Studio in town.

BUDDY
Remember when Kim did ballet?

PATTIE
Yeah, what a waste of money that was.
   (beat)
The tutu was cute though. Remember the tutu, Kimmy?

KIMBERLY
It chafed.

PATTIE
Mrs. Gigante says if I ever want the baby to take lessons at the Studio, I need to reserve a spot now because Miss Maxie is very popular.

KIMBERLY
It could be a boy, you know.

PATTIE
Boys take ballet.

BUDDY
Aw geez, you're gonna make him gay.

PATTIE
Oh shut up, you homophobe. I think *you're* gay.

BUDDY
I wish I was.

PATTIE
That's very nice. You wish you were gay, you wish you were deaf. Do you ever wish you were sober?

BUDDY
Eat shit, Pattie.

PATTIE
Oh! That's a nickel! Ya hear him, Kim? He said shit!

KIMBERLY
So did you.

PATTIE
What? Oh damnit! Wait, does damnit count?

KIMBERLY
Yeah.

PATTIE
Fuck.
   (*catches herself*)
Damnit!
   (*again*)
Shit!

BUDDY
Geez, it's like you've got Tourette's, Pattie. Chill out.

PATTIE
How many nickels was that?

KIMBERLY
One for Dad. Six for you.

BUDDY
Good goin'. We'll have that Jolly Jumper by Thursday.

PATTIE
Put in for me, I don't have any money.
> (BUDDY *digs in his pockets and puts seven nickels in the jar. Suddenly* PATTIE *gets a jolt. She sits up, worried.*)

BUDDY
What's the matter?

PATTIE
The baby kicked again.

BUDDY
That's okay. You *want* the baby to kick. Means it's active and healthy. It's a good thing.

PATTIE
Right. Okay.
> (*beat*)

This one's gonna be perfect, Bud. I can tell just by people's reactions to me. Do you remember in the grocery store last week? People would just look at me and smile. They love to see a pregnant woman. Especially the ladies. Why do you think they were all smiling?

KIMBERLY
Because you're fatter than they are.
> (KIMBERLY *gets up, goes to phone book and looks up a number.*)

PATTIE
> (*to* BUDDY)

They were smiling because they sense there's something special in here.
> (*pats her stomach*)

Isn't that right, baby?
> (KIMBERLY *dials phone number.*)

BUDDY
I'll make some pasta. You want some bow-tie pasta?

PATTIE
All right then, if I can't have a Zippy Fish.

BUDDY
Where my chef's hat? I can't cook without my hat.

PATTIE
It's in the cabinet, next to my Thorazine.

KIMBERLY
(*into the phone*)
Hi. Is Jeff McCracken there? . . . Kimberly Levaco.

BUDDY
I hope you're not calling that bonehead from the burger joint.

KIMBERLY
I'm on the phone!

(*Blackout.*)

Scene Four

(*Lights up in a library.* KIMBERLY *and* JEFF *talk over a table littered with their school bags, notebooks, and pencils.*)

JEFF
And I'm a member of The Junior Wordsmiths of America, an organization dedicated to the puzzleistic arts.

KIMBERLY
Oh. The puzzleistic arts.

JEFF
Yeah. You know, word-play games. Palindrome challenges. Spoonerisms. Anagrams are my specialty.

KIMBERLY
Which one's an anagram again?

JEFF
You scramble all the letters of something to spell out some-

thing else. Like the letters in George Washington can be re-arranged to spell out Sweet Groaning Hog.

KIMBERLY
Huh. You figured that out yourself?

JEFF
Yes I did. Some come in my monthly newsletter. Like Federal Government can be re-arranged to spell out Large Fervent Demon.

KIMBERLY
Right.

JEFF
And Mother-in-Law turns into Woman Hitler. My Dad loves that one.
(KIM *notices that* JEFF *wears a ring on a chain around his neck.*)

KIMBERLY
What's on that chain?

JEFF
A ring.

KIMBERLY
It's kinda girly.

JEFF
It's my mom's.

KIMBERLY
She lets you wear it?

JEFF
She left it to me.

KIMBERLY
Oh.
(KIMBERLY *takes this in.*)

JEFF
(reads from his notes)
So your disease is like Progeria without the dwarfism, the beaked nose, and the receded chin.

KIMBERLY
Yeah.

JEFF
And your body ages four times as fast as it should.

KIMBERLY
Four and a half.

JEFF
Right, so when you were four, you looked eighteen. And when you're twenty you'll look ninety.

KIMBERLY
Crazy, right?

JEFF
(*in books*)
And the average life expectancy is sixteen.
(*beat*)
Is that right?

KIMBERLY
Uh-huh.

JEFF
How old are *you*?

KIMBERLY
Can you do my name?

JEFF
What?

KIMBERLY
My name. Can you do an anagram of it?

JEFF
Oh . . . sure. I just wanna make sure I get the chromosome thing first.

KIMBERLY
Right. Okay, watch.
(*draws a diagram*)
You inherit an A *or* a B chromosome from Dad. And an A or

a B from Mom. A's are good, B's are bad. If you get two A's that's great. If you get one A and one B, you're just a carrier. But if you get two B's, you're screwed.

JEFF
You got two B's.

KIMBERLY
Correct.

JEFF
So if your parents ever have a baby, there's always a twenty-five percent chance the kid will have it.

KIMBERLY
Right.

JEFF
Guess they aren't gonna try that again.

KIMBERLY
(*beat*)
Now can you do it?
(*He doesn't remember.*)
The anagram of my name.

JEFF
Oh right. Yeah. But only if you time me.

KIMBERLY
All right.
(JEFF *grabs some paper and a pencil.*)

JEFF
(*writing her name down*)
Kimberly . . . and Levaco is L-E-V-A-C-O?

KIMBERLY
Yeah. Ready?

JEFF
Hold on.
(*gets set*)
Okay.

KIMBERLY
(looks at watch)
Go!

JEFF
(working on the anagram)
One C, right?

KIMBERLY
Yes.

(JEFF *works on the anagram through most of the following dialogue, barely looking up at* KIM.)

JEFF
I like to pull out the K's first because that's one of the hardest letters to use.

KIMBERLY
Oh yeah?

JEFF
Yeah. K's, J's, and Q's are the hardest.
(pause as he works)
You know, when I first saw you in the cafeteria, I thought you were a new lunch lady. Isn't that funny?
(no response)
Sorry. Are you sensitive?

KIMBERLY
No.

JEFF
That's good.
(pause while he works)
So you glad you moved to Bogota?

KIMBERLY
It's okay.

JEFF
And it's not weird for you?

KIMBERLY
Is what not weird for me?

ACT ONE

JEFF
To be in high school?

KIMBERLY
No. Why would that be weird?

JEFF
I mean . . . since the other kids ignore you?

KIMBERLY
I could ask you the same question.

JEFF
They don't ignore me. I *wish* they ignored me.

KIMBERLY
Oh yeah?

JEFF
(*slams down pencil proudly*)
Done!

KIMBERLY
Really?

JEFF
How fast was I?

KIMBERLY
(*checks watch*)
56 seconds.

JEFF
It would've been faster but I was carrying on a conversation at the same time.

KIMBERLY
What'd you get?

JEFF
Kimberly Levaco turns into . . . Cleverly Akimbo.
(*Pause. She's not impressed.*)
What's the matter?

KIMBERLY
What's Akimbo?

JEFF
It's . . . bent. You know, when your hands are on your hips, then your arms are *akimbo*.

KIMBERLY
(*still mulling it over*)
Cleverly akimbo.

JEFF
It's good. You should be happy. I did my grandmother's name and she got Arabian Beard.

(DEBRA, *a woman in her early 30's, approaches suspiciously. She's somewhat disheveled and rough around the edges. She carries a garbage bag filled with her belongings.*)

DEBRA
(*whispers*)
Kim. Hey.
(*They look over at the strange woman.*)

DEBRA
How you doin', Beautiful?

KIMBERLY
I'm fine.

DEBRA
God, I'm glad to see ya.

KIMBERLY
Where have you been?

DEBRA
You won't believe it. I was actually in a squat for a couple months, in Trenton.

KIMBERLY
A squat? What's a squat?

DEBRA
It's a terrible place, Kim. But the people are nice. And after that, I was living in the woods for a few weeks, but then my tent caught on fire, so I went back to Secaucus, but you guys

weren't there anymore, so I called Aunt Helen, and she wouldn't let me stay with her, but she told me you all took off to Bogota.
(*to* JEFF)
How you doin'?

JEFF

Good.

DEBRA

And so I came here, but you're not listed in the phone book, so I figured I'd wait in the library until you came by. And I knew you'd come by because I remembered you like to read so much. And so I've been here for 10 days.

KIMBERLY

You've been living in the library?

DEBRA

Yeah, keep it down though. They're real strict about the noise. It's comfortable. I sleep in the pillow room. At closing time I hide under the pile of bean-bag chairs. Haven't been caught yet.
(*to* JEFF)
What's your name?

JEFF

Jeff McCracken.

DEBRA

Nice to meet you. I'm Debra Watts. You gonna eat that cookie?

JEFF

(*looks at his snack*)
I guess not.

DEBRA

(*takes it*)
You don't mind, do ya? I haven't eaten in a couple days.
(*takes a bite and looks to* KIMBERLY)
I missed ya, kiddo.
(*to* JEFF)
Kimmy ever mention her Aunt Debra?

JEFF

No.

DEBRA
We're best buds, right Kimber?
  (*to* JEFF)
If you ever do anything to hurt her, I will fuck you up big time!
  (*beat, turns to* KIM)
I think your friend just shit his pants.

KIMBERLY
Debra, come on . . .

DEBRA
What? I'm sorry.
  (*to* JEFF)
You know I was just messin' with your head, right? You're a good kid. You want a handjob? I'm just kidding. I'm a dyke so I don't actually do that anymore. Unless ya got twenty bucks. You're not underage are ya?

JEFF
Yes.

DEBRA
Well the deal's off then. I've spent enough time in jail. You'll have to pleasure yourself, Dexter.

KIMBERLY
What are you *doing*?

DEBRA
I'm just playin' around. What happened, you don't like my jokes anymore? Wait, this isn't a date is it?

KIMBERLY
No.

DEBRA
Oh good, 'cause this kid's kinda freaky.
  (*to* JEFF)
Don't take offense though. I was a total outcast myself.

JEFF
That doesn't surprise me.

DEBRA
Hey, there ya go! Rising to the occasion!
  (*to* KIM)
He's a keeper.

KIMBERLY
Could I maybe meet you out front in a few minutes?

DEBRA
Hell no. I gotta go see a guy about something. Hey, how come you guys didn't tell me you were moving?

KIMBERLY
You disappeared.

DEBRA
You coulda left a note or something.

KIMBERLY
Dad seemed anxious to leave.

DEBRA
Yeah, me too. I understand.
   (*suddenly notices someone nearby*)
Shit.
   (*grabs a book and pretends to read*)

KIMBERLY
What's the matter?

DEBRA
That old lady's been giving me the stink-eye all day.

KIMBERLY
The librarian?

DEBRA
Yeah, she might be on to me. She caught me giving myself a splash-bath in the ladies' room this morning.

KIMBERLY
A what?

DEBRA
You know, just the vitals: the pits, the snatch.

JEFF
Ew.

DEBRA
   (*turns on* JEFF)
Hey kid, you have no idea how hard it is to be homeless!

JEFF
Sorry.
(*With the librarian out of sight,* DEBRA *starts rummaging through her garbage bag.*)

DEBRA
Hold on, I got ya somethin', Kimmy. For your birthday.

KIMBERLY
You did?

DEBRA
Don't sound so surprised.

JEFF
When's your birthday?

KIMBERLY
Today.

DEBRA
I found ya just in time.

JEFF
Why didn't you say anything?

DEBRA
(*hands her a badly gift-wrapped present*)
Sweet sixteen and never been kissed, right?

KIMBERLY
Shut up.

DEBRA
I wrapped it myself.

KIMBERLY
(*unwraps a conch shell*)
It's a shell.

JEFF
A conch shell.

KIMBERLY
What's it do?

DEBRA
You blow in it. See the hole in the end? It's like a horn.

KIMBERLY
Right.

DEBRA
I got it in Trenton off this crack-head Winnie. She used to own a hotel in Miami Beach.

JEFF
And now she lives in a squat?

DEBRA
Life takes awful turns, kid.
(*to* KIM)
That shell came all the way from Florida.

KIMBERLY
It's nice. Thank you.

DEBRA
You're welcome.
(*beat*)
So. I'm gonna need the address.

KIMBERLY
What address?

DEBRA
To the house.

KIMBERLY
Our house?

DEBRA
Come on, Kimmy. Don't play with me.

KIMBERLY
I can't. I'm not supposed to.

DEBRA
Why not? Because of your Dad? I'm family. You think he wants me to sleep on the streets?

KIMBERLY
Probably.

DEBRA
But *you* don't. You've got heart, right? Which reminds me, I'm gonna need your help, Kim. Can you help me with something?

KIMBERLY

I don't know.

DEBRA

It's something I've been thinking about. Something good for us both. You'll like it. Maybe we can work your friend in.

JEFF

No thanks.

DEBRA

Gimme the address wouldja?

(KIMBERLY *reluctantly writes it down.*)

DEBRA

Thanks, gorgeous. Leave the front door unlocked and I'll talk to ya tonight.

KIMBERLY

Okay.

DEBRA

In the meantime, if anyone asks, you didn't see me.
(*turns to* JEFF)
You neither.

JEFF

All right.

DEBRA

Peace out, y'all.

(DEBRA *slips away suddenly. The kids look after her.*)

KIMBERLY

I am *so* sorry.

JEFF

That's okay, my aunt's a lesbian, too.

KIMBERLY

Really?

JEFF

Really. She's not nearly as inappropriate as your aunt, though.

KIMBERLY

Yeah, that's kinda her thing.

JEFF
She used to live with you?

KIMBERLY
Yeah, in Secaucus. She slept in our basement. But then she did something so we had to move.

JEFF
What'd she do?

KIMBERLY
I don't know. They don't really talk about it.

JEFF
Huh. I have cousins in Secaucus.

KIMBERLY
(*beat*)
Oh. You do?
(*pause*)
You know what? I should be going.
(*starts to gather her stuff together*)

JEFF
What's the matter?

KIMBERLY
I have to feed my mom.

JEFF
Your mom?

KIMBERLY
She has Carpal Tunnel. I'll call you though.

JEFF
I'm not gonna say anything. I never even see them. They're very distant cousins.

KIMBERLY
Well that's good. I really gotta go though.

JEFF
All right.

KIMBERLY
I'll see you tomorrow.
(KIMBERLY *exits with her book bag.*)

Scene Five

(Lights up on the kitchen table. It's late at night. PATTIE *is talking into the tape recorder again. The jar on the table is already half-filled with nickels. The table is set for dinner.)*

PATTIE

And one of my best friends was Mr. Hicks. He lived next door to us in Secaucus. He brought me cabbage from his garden. You would've liked Mr. Hicks. When I wasn't feeling well, he'd run to the corner and buy my cigarettes for me. He was kind like that. He'd do whatever you asked him to.
  (A conch shell blows loudly offstage.)

PATTIE

What in God's name . . .
  (Again, the conch shell blows offstage.)

PATTIE

Kim, what are you doing?

KIMBERLY

  (off)
I'm blowing my conch shell.

PATTIE

Well cut it out, you'll wake the neighbors!
  (to tape)
I don't know about you, baby, but I'm so hungry I could chew off my own arm.
  (calls off to KIM*)*
Kim! Me and the baby need some food!

KIMBERLY

  (off)
I'll be there in a second!

PATTIE
Where'd you get a conch shell?!

KIMBERLY
(*off*)
Don Ho. He spoke at our school today.

PATTIE
That is a lie. You better not have stolen that thing.
(KIMBERLY *enters wearing pajamas. She's been trying on make-up.*)

KIMBERLY
I didn't steal it.

PATTIE
Make us some cereal.

KIMBERLY
You can't wait for Dad?

PATTIE
It's ten o'clock. I'll get a long white beard waiting for that no-show. I don't know why you bothered setting the table.

KIMBERLY
(*goes to make a bowl of Frosted Flakes*)
He said he'd make dinner.

PATTIE
Yeah well, he-said-he-said. He's said a lot of things over the years, and ninety percent of it was bullshit.

KIMBERLY
Jar.

PATTIE
Shit.

KIMBERLY
Mom.

PATTIE
I'm sorry. I'm trying. Your Dad put some nickels aside. Pop 'em in.
(KIM *tosses a couple nickels in the jar, then looks up at the clock.*)

KIMBERLY
Where do you think he is?
(*pours milk over the cereal*)

PATTIE
Oh, he's probably face down in a bowl of peanuts somewhere.
(KIMBERLY *sits down with the cereal bowl and feeds her mother the way one might feed a baby.*)

PATTIE
I love Don Ho. Your father used to say he was gonna take me to Hawaii to meet him. Of course that never happened.

KIMBERLY
Maybe he'll surprise you some day. You never know.

PATTIE
Yeah you do. Sometimes, Kim, you actually do know. I'm never seeing Hawaii.
(*beat*)
Hey, I did that spinning needle on a string trick. It said I'm having another girl. Exciting, right?

KIMBERLY
How'd you thread a needle?

PATTIE
It took an hour and a half, but I did it.
(*into the tape recorder*)
Persevere in life, baby girl. That's another good lesson I'm passing on to you.
(*back to* KIMBERLY)
I was just telling your sister about Mr. Hicks. Remember that nice old man?

KIMBERLY
Dad said he was a pervert who kept stacks of dirty magazines in his basement.

PATTIE
Kimberly, don't say—!
(*hits stop on tape-recorder and then rewinds*)
Now I have to rewind and record over that. You are not gonna say mean things about Mr. Hicks on my tape. He brought me cabbage!

(*hits record again*)
As I was saying . . . Do you remember Mr. Hicks, Kimberly?

KIMBERLY

Vaguely.

PATTIE

Wasn't it funny how he called you The Duchess?

KIMBERLY

It wasn't that funny.

PATTIE

Yes, he called you The Duchess, and me Hiawatha. He was such a comical little man.
(*Sounds of someone sneaking in the front*)

KIMBERLY

Is that him?

PATTIE

He better have his shoes in his hand.
(*giggles*)
Like in the cartoons, you know?

DEBRA

(*sneaks in*)
Anyone home?

PATTIE

Aw hell.

DEBRA

Hey, Sista. Ya miss me?

PATTIE

Not at all. Go away, Debra.

DEBRA

Aw come on, you don't mean it.

PATTIE

Yes I do. Things have been very quiet around here. You have to leave.

DEBRA

Nice place. Except for that wallpaper. Yikes. It's like you live in a giant thermos.

PATTIE
I mean it, Deb, you cannot stay here.

DEBRA
Don't worry, it won't be for long.

PATTIE
That's what you said the last time, and you stayed for six years.

DEBRA
I got a few things out front to bring in.

PATTIE
What things?

DEBRA
I'll keep 'em in the basement with me, relax.

PATTIE
Buddy's head is gonna explode.

DEBRA
Don't even tell him I'm here. I'll be like a mouse.
(*goes back out front*)

PATTIE
How'd she even find us?

KIMBERLY
Who knows?

PATTIE
Stay away from her, Kim. Do me that favor. We'll just pretend she doesn't exist, okay?
(*suddenly notices*)
Are you wearing lipstick?

KIMBERLY
Yeah.

PATTIE
Why?

KIMBERLY
I was just trying it on. I wanted to see what it'd look like.

PATTIE
And rouge?

KIMBERLY
A little bit.

PATTIE
I don't like it. You look like a made-up corpse.
(DEBRA *enters with large cans of chemicals. She crosses to the basement.*)

PATTIE
What are those?

DEBRA
They're just chemicals I need.

PATTIE
Chemicals? Why do you need chemicals?

DEBRA
Which way's the basement?

KIMBERLY
That way.

PATTIE
You better not be building a bomb down there.

DEBRA
(*exiting to basement*)
I'm not building a bomb.

PATTIE
(*into the tape recorder*)
That's your Aunt Debra. Never loan her money.

KIMBERLY
(*looks up at the clock again*)
Think he'll be home by midnight?

PATTIE
Why, he gonna turn into a pumpkin? What's with you?

KIMBERLY
(*holds up cereal spoon*)
Another bite.

PATTIE
Another bite for the baby girl.
   (*baby talk*)
Da widdle baby eats it up wid a gweat big spoon and poops in her pants like a good baby should.

KIMBERLY
Mom?

PATTIE
Yes?

KIMBERLY
Can we just be normal for a few minutes?
   (*beat*)
Can you just ask me how school was or something?

PATTIE
You're such a stick-in-the-mud, ya know it? Criticizing my mothering skills.
   (*into tape recorder*)
That buzz-kill you hear is your sister Kimberly. I can't wait for you to come out and tell her to lighten up.
   (DEBRA *crosses from basement.*)

PATTIE
Remember Kim had such a sour puss when she was born?

DEBRA
I was incarcerated the last time you gave birth.
   (*exits*)

PATTIE
Oh that's right. Well she *did*. We called her grumpy-face.
   (*to* KIM)
Cute, right?
   (*off her reaction*)
Hey, I know what'll cheer you up. You wanna name the baby?

KIMBERLY
No, I don't wanna name the baby.

PATTIE
Aw, come on, it'll be fun. You have such a good imagination. Remember that Don Ho thing you said? That was clever. *Pleeease*.

KIMBERLY
God, okay. How about . . .

PATTIE
Pick something good.

KIMBERLY
I'm feeling like she's a . . . Carmelita?

PATTIE
(*pleased*)
Oh yes. That's a pretty name. I'm gonna have me a Spanish baby. Little Carmelita. My bonita baby.

KIMBERLY
You like it?

PATTIE
Very much. Thank you.
  (DEBRA *crosses to basement carrying stacks of glue traps.*)

PATTIE
Hey, Kim just named the baby!

DEBRA
Did you show her the shell I got for your birthday, Kimmy?
  (PATTIE *looks over to* KIM. *Silence.*)

DEBRA
What'd your mom get ya? Something lame I'll bet.
  (*off* PATTIE'S *look*)
What?

PATTIE
I forgot.

DEBRA
You forgot her birthday?

PATTIE
Don't start with me, Debra!

DEBRA
You didn't forget.
  (*heads into basement*)

PATTIE

I did so!

(*The phone rings.* PATTIE *and* KIM *freeze. They look at each other. The phone continues to ring.* KIM *goes over and answers it.*)

KIMBERLY

(*answers phone*)
Hello? . . . Uh-huh . . . Uh-huh . . . Fine.
(*hangs up*)

PATTIE

(*beat*)
Car problems?

(KIMBERLY *starts putting the dishes from the table back into the cabinet. She spends much of the following dialogue quietly clearing the table.*)

PATTIE

I'm sorry I forgot, honey. I think the cancer's spread to my memory cells.

KIMBERLY

You don't have cancer.

PATTIE

Are you a doctor?

KIMBERLY

No, Mom, I'm not a doctor.

PATTIE

Then don't tell me what I do or don't have.
(*beat*)
I'm gonna die, Kim. It's sad, but you need to be prepared. People pass away, you know. Suddenly they're gone forever. Look at Mr. Hicks. One day he's bringing me cabbages from his garden, the next day he drops dead.
(*to* DEBRA, *who passes from basement to exit house*)
Remember when Mr. Hicks dropped dead, Debra?

DEBRA

Jesus, Pattie, give it a rest. Your mouth is like a lawn mower.

PATTIE
You'll miss my mouth when I'm dead.

DEBRA
I don't think so.
(*exits*)

PATTIE
(*to* KIMBERLY)
You'll miss me, too. Because I'm a fixture in your life. You'll have to actually remind yourself I'm gone. That's how it was when your Nana died. I kept forgetting she was dead. I'd see a sale at the supermarket and think, "Oh Ma, should get down there for those pork chops." And then I'd remember, "Oh yeah, she's dead." You get so used to someone being there, it takes your body a long time to adjust.
(KIMBERLY *continues to clear the table.*)

PATTIE
Like when you move a lamp, and you keep going to the same place to turn it on in the dark, even though you moved it across the room weeks ago. Or do you remember when Cinnamon died, and we still kept going to put the table scraps into his dog-bowl? We were just so used to it? That's how it's gonna be when I'm gone. You'll have to keep reminding yourself that I'm not here anymore.

KIMBERLY
Or visa versa.

PATTIE
(*pause*)
You take that back.

KIMBERLY
Sixteen is just an average, Mom. Just because it's my birthday doesn't mean—

PATTIE
(*stops her*)
I was not talking about *you*. I was talking about *myself*.

KIMBERLY
As always.

PATTIE
I'm the one who's falling apart, after all. You're so self-involved.
(DEBRA *enters dragging a mailbox.*)

PATTIE
What is that?

DEBRA
It's a mailbox, Pattie.

PATTIE
I know it's a mailbox! Jesus Christ!

DEBRA
You wanna help me with this, Kim?

KIMBERLY
Sure.
(KIM *goes to mailbox.*)

PATTIE
You can't steal mailboxes. That is a federal offense.
(DEBRA *and* KIMBERLY *cross to basement with the mailbox.*)

DEBRA
How was school?

KIMBERLY
Good. We had a mock debate.

PATTIE
Hey, we decided to ignore Debra, remember, Kim?

KIMBERLY
I lobbied for animal rights.

PATTIE
I'm sorry I forgot your birthday.

DEBRA
Did your side win?

KIMBERLY
Yeah. We won.
(*They've gone to the basement.*)

PATTIE

I'll make your father get a cake! Kim, you didn't wipe my mouth! . . . Kim?! . . . Fine!
(*wipes her mouth with her bandages*)
Come back! I'll try to be normal! Kim?!
(*pause*)
You see how they treat me, Carmelita? You have the evidence right there. All of it, *caught on tape!*

(*Lights crossfade to . . .*)

Scene Six

(BUDDY's *car. He's driving.* KIMBERLY *is in the passenger's seat.* JEFF *is in the back.*)

JEFF

Thanks for the ride to school, Mr. Levaco.

BUDDY

Uh-huh.

JEFF

You really didn't have to offer.

BUDDY

You were standing in front of my car.

JEFF

Yeah, I was just gonna ask Kimberly a couple more questions before I presented my paper today.

BUDDY

You shouldn't stand in people's driveways like that. You're gonna get yourself run over.

JEFF

Thanks for the tip, Mr. L.

BUDDY

(*notices* KIM)
What's the matter?

KIMBERLY
My back is sore. My shoulders too.

BUDDY
Huh. Those are new. Maybe we can go to the clinic tomorrow.

JEFF
This is a nice car.

BUDDY
What are you talking about? It's a total wreck.

JEFF
Yeah, but I usually take the bus to school. This is much more comfortable. No one's spitting at me.

BUDDY
It's early yet.

(JEFF *laughs nervously.*)

JEFF
Do you have your license yet, Kim?

KIMBERLY
No.

JEFF
I got mine two months ago. But my Dad won't let me touch the car. Says I'm accident prone. I think I'm a pretty good driver, though. Want me to take the wheel for a couple blocks, Mr. Levaco?

BUDDY
No, just keep quiet.

JEFF
My Dad would drive me to school himself, but he works the night shift. He gets home real late and then sleeps in.

KIMBERLY
Yeah, my Dad gets in real late too sometimes. Last night it was almost three, wasn't it?

JEFF
You work the night shift too, Mr. Levaco?

BUDDY
No, I don't.

KIMBERLY
Musta been hard getting up this morning.

BUDDY
I managed.

JEFF
You know, if you rearrange all the letters in Snooze Alarms, you come up with Alas, No More Z's.

BUDDY
Huh. That's weird.

JEFF
Where do you work, Mr. Levaco?

BUDDY
The Chevron Station on Palisades Ave.
   (JEFF *writes something in his notebook.*)

JEFF
Are you the guy in the booth?

BUDDY
Yeah, I'm the guy in the booth.

JEFF
My Dad works in a booth, too. He collects tolls on the turnpike.

BUDDY
That's a lousy job. Breathing in those fumes all day.

JEFF
He likes it.

KIMBERLY
   (*under her breath*)
"Oh sure I can cook dinner. That's a great idea."

BUDDY
What?

KIMBERLY
Forget it.

BUDDY
If you have something to say, Kim—

KIMBERLY
I don't. Just go faster. You drive like an old man.

BUDDY
(to JEFF)
Kim's upset because I went out for a few beers after work instead of making dinner.

KIMBERLY
Dad, shut up.

BUDDY
She thinks I should stay home and smoke pipes and wear sweaters.

KIMBERLY
That's not what I think.

BUDDY
Then why are you being all pissy?

KIMBERLY
I'm not. Drop it.

BUDDY
Don't worry about what time I get in. I'm the grown-up, not you. So mind your own business.

KIMBERLY
I didn't even say anything.

BUDDY
Yeah, you kinda did actually. Are you showing off for your boyfriend?

KIMBERLY
Dad—

BUDDY
Kim—
(beat)
Just cut it out.

JEFF
(*looking up from his notebook*)
Oh No, Vast Cretin.
(BUDDY *and* KIMBERLY *look at him blankly.*)
Chevron Station. Its anagram. Oh No, Vast Cretin.

BUDDY
All right, enough with the Jumbles.

JEFF
Sorry. Once you start, it's hard to stop. It's like heroin.

BUDDY
Heroin?

JEFF
A.K.A. smack, brown, junk, "H." My older brother's in re-hab. He crashed my dad's Moped.

BUDDY
(*to* KIM)
You finish that glaucoma paper?

KIMBERLY
Yes.

JEFF
You know, Bonnie Gigante picked glaucoma, too.

KIMBERLY
So?

JEFF
I'm just saying.

BUDDY
Hey, can you get us free burgers?

JEFF
Free burgers?

BUDDY
Yeah. Since you work at Zippy Burger? Seeing as I gave you a ride?

JEFF
Oh . . . I . . . I'm not really allowed to do that.

BUDDY
You can't slip us a vanilla shake on the sly?

JEFF
Well, they count the cups, so . . . They'd know one was missing.

BUDDY
Oh, I see how it is. Okay then.

JEFF
Hey Kimberly, you ever play Dungeons and Dragons?

KIMBERLY
No.

JEFF
Do you wanna, though? I could be the Dungeon Master.

KIMBERLY
It's a game?

JEFF
Yeah, you go on an adventure, and you could be like an Elvin Cleric or a Paladin or something. Wanna see my dice?
(*holds up velvet pouch*)

KIMBERLY
Sure
(KIMBERLY *takes the bag and looks at the multi-colored dice inside.*)

JEFF
They're for rolling hit point damage and stuff, like if you get attacked by a Hobgoblin.

BUDDY
That game's for Devil worshipers. You're not roping her into that shit.

JEFF
What? It's not for Devil worshipers.

BUDDY
You go to graveyards and sacrifice cats and whatnot. I've seen it on the news. It makes kids crazy, and they kill themselves.

JEFF
You've got it mixed up with something else, Mr. Levaco. This is just a fantasy role-playing game.

BUDDY
Try those Pop-O-Matic games instead. Good clean fun.

KIMBERLY
These dice are so cool.

JEFF
You wanna play?

BUDDY
She's not playing.

KIMBERLY
(*holds up a die*)
Look at this dice, Dad.

JEFF
The singular of dice is die. It's a die.

KIMBERLY
Look at this die, Dad.

JEFF
It's twelve-sided.

BUDDY
See, it's like a pentagram or something.

KIMBERLY
It's just a die.

JEFF
You could play D and D too, Mr. Levaco.

BUDDY
No. No one is playing D and D!
(*pause*)
I'm sorry to yell, Jeff, but I feel strongly about this issue.

JEFF
Not a problem. My Dad yells, too. So does my brother when he needs more methadone. So I've gotten used to yelling.

BUDDY
Good for you.

JEFF
(*beat*)
I do get a discount.

BUDDY
A discount?

JEFF
At the Zippy Burger. So, if you wanted that, I could probably say I was buying the food for myself.

BUDDY
Well now you're talkin'. Maybe I'll take you up on that offer.

JEFF
If you do, can I have a ride tomorrow, too?

BUDDY
I don't see why not. So long as you keep quiet. Discounted burgers. I bet they taste better when you're not paying full price. Right, Kim?

KIMBERLY
You missed my birthday.

BUDDY
(*beat*)
I know. I talked to your mother. I'm getting a cake over at Lambert's tonight.

KIMBERLY
(*beat*)
That's it?

BUDDY
Whadaya want me to say? This stuff happens. I don't think my old man ever remembered my birthday.

KIMBERLY
How comforting.

BUDDY
I'm sorry, honey. But you know how crazy it's been with the move and the new job and the baby and everything.

KIMBERLY
(*peeved*)
Uh-huh.

BUDDY
Oh for godsakes you're gettin' your freakin' cake, now cut me some slack!
(*beat*)
Between you and your mother . . .

JEFF
(*after a pause*)
So, did you work at a gas station in Secaucus too, Mr. Levaco?

BUDDY
What?

JEFF
When you lived in Secaucus? Was there a Chevron there, too?

BUDDY
Who said we lived in Secaucus?

JEFF
Kimberly did.
(BUDDY *shoots her a look.*)

KIMBERLY
It just came up.

BUDDY
Right, it just came up.

KIMBERLY
I didn't say anything. I just said we lived there.

JEFF
Don't worry, she didn't give away any family secrets, Mr. Levaco.

BUDDY
What are you talking about?

JEFF
Nothing.

BUDDY
We don't have any family secrets.

JEFF
I didn't say you did.

BUDDY
What'd you say to him?

KIMBERLY
Nothing.

BUDDY
Are you punishing me?

KIMBERLY
No, Dad—

BUDDY
What'd I say about talking to people?

JEFF
We had to talk, for my paper.

BUDDY
And I thought I told you Kim was busy?

JEFF
You did, but then—

BUDDY
I thought I told you to pick another disease?

JEFF
Kimberly called *me*.

BUDDY
No one needs to know my family business.

JEFF
I didn't ask about the family, it was just—

BUDDY
I'm gonna tell you something, Jeff, because I was a boy and I was sixteen once, and I know what's going on here.

KIMBERLY
Dad, cut it out.

BUDDY
You are not gonna get all chatty with Kim and start feeling her tits.

KIMBERLY
Oh my *god*.

JEFF
Mr. Levaco—

BUDDY
I know how the hormones work.

KIMBERLY
Shut *up*.

BUDDY
I know what this *discount burger* business is about.

JEFF
I just wanted a ride to school.

BUDDY
I knew how to warm up the Dads. I knew how to make conversation and be the nice kid.

JEFF
That's not what I'm doing.

BUDDY
But I was bright enough to talk about baseball and not some Satanic role-playing game.

JEFF
It's not Satanic.

BUDDY
I knew the *right* way to get into a girl's pants.

JEFF
I'm not getting into anyone's pants.

BUDDY
You've got *that* right, Jeffrey! Now not another word about Secaucus! No Secaucus, no D and D and no tit-touching! I mean it!

KIMBERLY
I hate you. I hope you drink yourself sick and crash this fucking car! I hope you swerve off a cliff and this shit-box explodes and you die, you mother-fucker!

(*silence*)

JEFF
(*looking out the window*)
Oh look. We're here.

(*Blackout.*)

Scene Seven

(*Lights up in the library.* DEBRA *hustles* JEFF *into the room.*)

DEBRA
Kim didn't tell you about the meeting?

JEFF
No. And really, I don't think I should be attending any *meetings* with you people.

DEBRA
Oh yeah? Why's that?

JEFF
Because Mr. Levaco got mad at me this morning, and I don't even know what I did. But the main thing he said was I shouldn't know too much about his family, so I think I should just stay away.

DEBRA
You know what your problem is? You worry too much. Anyone ever tell you that?

JEFF
Yes. That's why I take anxiety medication.
(KIMBERLY *enters.*)

DEBRA
You're late. And I thought I told you to fill the kid in?

KIMBERLY
(*surprised to see* JEFF)
Oh. Actually . . .

DEBRA
Why is it always up to me to be the responsible one?
(*motions* KIM *to a chair*)
Sit. I got some stuff in the Xerox machine. Don't move until I get back. Neither of ya.
(*exits*)

KIMBERLY
You should probably escape while you can.

JEFF
That's okay. She'll just catch me and drag me back here.
(*They sit in silence. After an awkward pause . . .*)

JEFF
I liked your glaucoma paper by the way. It was way better than Bonnie Gigante's.

KIMBERLY
You think?

JEFF
Yeah, you had that eyeball diagram and everything. It was very thorough.

KIMBERLY
Thanks.

JEFF
(*another pause*)
So, are you like . . . mad at me?

KIMBERLY
No.

JEFF
About my paper?

KIMBERLY
No, it was good.

JEFF
Because you looked weird after I read it in class.

KIMBERLY
No, it was a good paper.

JEFF
Then how come you ate lunch by yourself?

KIMBERLY
I was just reading.

JEFF
I thought you were mad at me.

KIMBERLY
I wasn't. I just . . . I thought you were done, so . . .

JEFF
Done? With lunch?

KIMBERLY
With the paper. Since you were done writing it, I thought . . .

JEFF
You thought I wouldn't have lunch with you?

KIMBERLY
I don't know.

JEFF
I thought you were mad about the paper, or your Dad or something.

KIMBERLY
My Dad?

JEFF
Or embarrassed. Since he told me not touch you and kiss you and stuff.

KIMBERLY
Oh, no I wasn't— I don't really wanna talk about that.

JEFF
Because I was thinking that if you wanted me to, I'd do it anyway.

KIMBERLY
What?

JEFF
I know it's his job to be protective and everything, but you might want to do something that he thinks you don't want to do. So if you wanted to like be kissed or whatever, then I would do it.
(*beat*)
As a friend, you know?
(*silence*)
Like if you just wanted someone to practice on.
(*beat*)
But not if you didn't want to, obviously. I'm just saying. I'm not afraid of your Dad. I mean I *am*, but I'm assuming you wouldn't tell him, so in that case I wouldn't be. Afraid of him, I mean.

(KIMBERLY *is too overwhelmed to speak. She has a giddy, mortified, thrilled expression on her face.*)

JEFF
Are you mad?

KIMBERLY
No.

JEFF
Because that's not why I've been hanging out with you or anything. I wasn't even thinking about it until your Dad brought it up. So . . . I don't know. I guess . . . if you ever want to, just let me know.

KIMBERLY
Okay.

JEFF
(*beat*)
Okay, you'll let me know? Or okay, right now?

KIMBERLY
Okay, I'll let you know.

JEFF
Okay.

KIMBERLY
It's just . . . She's gonna come back, so . . .

JEFF
Oh, right. I see. Cool.

(DEBRA *re-enters with checks and Xeroxes.*)

DEBRA
All set. Now listen up, because the plan's genius. You know what check-washing is?

JEFF
This is the sort of thing I think Mr. Levaco was talking about. I really shouldn't get involved with any kind of *check-washing plans*.

KIMBERLY
He doesn't wanna do it.

DEBRA
Just hear me out. It's the end of month, right? So everyone's paying bills, popping 'em in the mail. Gas, cable, whatever. So last night, I unbolted the mailbox outside Krapp's Liquor Store and dragged it home.

JEFF
You stole a mailbox?

DEBRA
Cool, right? And then Kim and I got these glue traps, you know, for mice . . .

KIMBERLY
(*to* JEFF)
I just helped a little.

DEBRA
And we tied strings through them and lowered them into the

mailbox, you know, like we were fishing, and we pulled up all these envelopes. And guess what was inside most of 'em.

JEFF

Checks?

DEBRA

Exactly. Checks I just Xeroxed on that machine over there with a roll of dimes I stole out of ol' Stink-Eye's purse.
(*points*)

JEFF

I'm getting acid-stomach.

DEBRA

And in our basement is a solution I made with a recipe I got off the internet. It said I mix this amount of Clorox with a splash of so and so, and when I drop the checks into the solution, guess what's gonna happen?

JEFF

The ink will come off?

DEBRA

Right! Whatever people wrote in will magically disappear, and I'll have a stack of blank checks. And since I Xeroxed the checks before I washed them . . .

JEFF

You still have the signatures.

DEBRA

And I've always been a first-class forger. Did two years in the Georgia Pen thanks to my outstanding forgeries.

KIMBERLY

She has this plan to rewrite all the checks.

DEBRA

And they'll look totally believable.

KIMBERLY

But she wants to make them out to you.

JEFF

To me?

KIMBERLY
I told her you probably didn't wanna do it.

JEFF
Why would the checks be made out to me?

DEBRA
You have a bank account, don't you?

JEFF
Yeah at First National, but there's only forty bucks in it.

DEBRA
Right now there's forty bucks, but how about we fill that puppy up?

KIMBERLY
She said we'd get a cut of the money.

DEBRA
I give you the new checks tomorrow, you go in with Kimberly. Kim pretends to be your grandmother—

KIMBERLY
I haven't agreed to all this. It's still hypothetical.

DEBRA
She says, "This is my grandson and he's just had a birthday and he'd like to cash some of his birthday checks." And they make sure you have an account, which you do, and they hand you all the cash. They won't even blink. Grandmother, little kid. Piece of cake. I take my half of the dough and hop a bus to Miami. My friend Winnie-the-crack-head says it's paradise down there.

JEFF
Can't we get in trouble?

DEBRA
No, you're kids. You can't get into trouble.

JEFF
But my brother was in a Juvenile Detention Center and—

DEBRA
Look, this is very safe.

JEFF
I can't do it. My dad'd kill me.

DEBRA
Ya buy him a tie.

JEFF
He doesn't wear ties.

DEBRA
Some tube socks then. Whatever he needs, you buy it. He'll love ya for it.

JEFF
(*considering it*)
He *does* need a new Moped.

DEBRA
There ya go, a Moped then!

KIMBERLY
I don't know, Aunt Debra.

DEBRA
Don't go backing out on me, Kim. He's starting to come 'round. And you promised.

KIMBERLY
I said maybe.

DEBRA
(*to* JEFF)
See what you're doing?! You're scaring Kim! Tell her it's a good idea!

JEFF
Well, I'll do it if she wants me to, but I don't think she does.

KIMBERLY
He's right, I don't. It's too much.

DEBRA
It's not too much! You owe me this! Who brought you to that bowling alley all those times? And the roller rink?! I did for *you*, now you do for *me*. That's how life works!

KIMBERLY

I know, but—

DEBRA

I've had it rough, Kim, you *know* that. You're gonna begrudge me a bus ticket? Because that's all I need. And I'll be good once I'm there, I promise. I'll start a new life. I'll get a straight job on the beach, selling slushies or something.

KIMBERLY

You can get a job *here* and earn a little money, go to Miami later.

DEBRA

I don't have time for later! My whole life has been later! I'm gonna get some crap-job at Wal-Mart and *wait* for things to get good? While years go by, and I get fat, and never get to Miami? That ain't me, Kimmy. I'm sorry.

KIMBERLY

It wouldn't be years.

DEBRA

Yes it would! For me, it would. I get trapped.

KIMBERLY

You get arrested. It's not the same thing.

DEBRA

I don't wanna wait anymore. I'm not a kid. I know what life does now. It flies right by ya. And the good things go with it. They don't stop to land in your lap. You gotta *grab* the good stuff, otherwise it's gone. And when it's gone, it don't come back, believe me.
   (*beat*)
Come on, Kimmy. Help me out. Please.

KIMBERLY

   (*pause*)
Okay.
   (*turns to* JEFF)
I think we should do it.
   (*The lights change.*)

Scene Eight

(*In the dark, sounds of* BUDDY *sneaking into the house, drunk. He knocks stuff over.*)

BUDDY

Shit . . . oopsy . . . another nickel.
(*giggles*)

(*Lights come up on him at* KIM's *bedroom door with a cake box and a shopping bag.* KIM *pretends to be asleep in her bed.* BUDDY *whispers.*)

BUDDY

Kim? . . . pssst . . . Kim honey . . .
(*edges into her room*)
You awake?

KIMBERLY

No.

BUDDY

Kim . . .
(*sits on the edge of* KIM's *bed*)
I'm sorry, Sweetie.
(*pause*)
Kim.

KIMBERLY

What?

BUDDY

I'm sorry.
(*holds up box*)
I got your cake. It's a little smooshed on the side. But I bet it still tastes good.

KIMBERLY

Dad, go to bed.

BUDDY

(*holds up bag*)
Plus I brought a present.

KIMBERLY
You're drunk.
(BUDDY *pulls a Trouble game from the bag.*)

BUDDY
It's a board game. Wanna play?

KIMBERLY
No.

BUDDY
It's the game of Trouble. It's a Pop-O-Matic game.

KIMBERLY
Dad—

BUDDY
Come on, Kimmy. Get up and play Trouble.
(*starts setting up the game board on the floor*)
Your Mom and I used to play this when we first got married. It's a good game.

KIMBERLY
I'm tired.

BUDDY
You're always tired. Now come sit here and help me set up.
(KIMBERLY *moves to the floor and helps him set up the Trouble board.* DEBRA *appears in the doorway. She clicks on the light.*)

DEBRA
Oh thank Christ, I thought the Feds found my mailbox.

BUDDY
(*beat*)
What is this?

DEBRA
How ya doin', Buddy?

BUDDY
What are you doing here?

DEBRA
You look good. Ya been workin' out?

BUDDY
Look, I don't know how you found us—

DEBRA
It *was* a challenge.

BUDDY
You gotta leave. I'm not kidding, Debra.

DEBRA
Now don't have a conniption.

BUDDY
And what the hell did you do to— You know what? I don't even wanna know. Just get out of here. You're gonna get us thrown in the pokey.

DEBRA
Pattie said I could stay. Didn't she, Kim?

BUDDY
Well, Pattie's not paying the rent, now screw.

DEBRA
(*suddenly notices*)
Ooo, a Pop-O-Matic game. Can I play?

BUDDY
Shhh, you'll wake her up!

KIMBERLY
(*referring to Trouble game*)
I'm the blue guys. What are you, Dad?

BUDDY
(*to* DEBRA)
You owe me a stereo by the way.

DEBRA
Kim, you should be asleep. We have a big day tomorrow.

BUDDY
What big day?

DEBRA
Hey, what's that? Cake? About time.

BUDDY
Okay, get out, Debra. I'm serious.

DEBRA
I love cake. I'll get the forks.
(*rushes off*)

BUDDY
Why do I bother? I'm like the guy on the hill pushin' the rock.

KIMBERLY
Was he drunk too?

BUDDY
Hey, that's not . . . You shouldn't say things like that.
(*beat*)
Besides . . . Tonight was my last hurrah.

KIMBERLY
Oh yeah?

BUDDY
Yeah. I was thinking . . . you know, about how you wished I would die. Remember you said that, about the car exploding? And I thought, "Well, that can't be a good thing for a daughter to say." So if you want me to stop, I promise to stop.

KIMBERLY
Uh-huh.

BUDDY
Have I ever promised before?

KIMBERLY
No.

BUDDY
All right then. See? How about Saturday we go to Six Flags Safari?

KIMBERLY
Okay.

(DEBRA *comes back in with forks, plates, and a knife.*)

DEBRA
This reminds me of the old days. My Dad staggering in loaded, waking me up to play Parcheesi over a slice of cake. I'm green. I'm always green in these games.

(DEBRA *cuts into the cake.*)

BUDDY
Debra, we didn't even sing.

(PATTIE *appears in a nightgown.*)

DEBRA
Uh-oh.

PATTIE
(*looks up at the clock*)
What time is it?

BUDDY
Oh. Hi, honey. Did we wake you?

PATTIE
You're playing a game?

BUDDY
I know it's late, but—

PATTIE
How come no one asked me to play?
(*no response*)
I like games too, you know.

KIMBERLY
You wanna play, Mom?

PATTIE
(*pause*)
May I be yellow?

KIMBERLY	BUDDY	DEBRA
Yeah, sure. No one's picked yellow yet.	Have a seat right here next to our guest of honor.	One more ass to kick. Like when we were kids.

PATTIE
(*joins them*)
Oh, and you got the cake.

DEBRA
It's lopsided.

BUDDY
I hit a pothole.

KIMBERLY
You want a piece?

PATTIE
I better not. My diabetes.

DEBRA
What diabetes?

BUDDY
Debra showed up again.

PATTIE
I know. She's like a bad rash.

BUDDY
I bought you a gift. Look, an electric toothbrush.
(*pulls electric toothbrush from bag*)
I thought this might be easier to manage. Better than the regular toothbrush. Since you have the bandages.

DEBRA
You know what we need? Music.
(DEBRA *gets up to put on the radio.* KIMBERLY *and* BUDDY *eat their cake.*)

PATTIE
Thank you for the toothbrush, Buddy.

BUDDY
I also got something for the baby. I just gotta plug it in.

PATTIE
Isn't that sweet?

DEBRA
How come I didn't get a gift? You got everybody something except me?

BUDDY
You got my stereo. That's gift enough.

(DEBRA *tunes in to a zippy swing era song.*)

DEBRA
How's that for music?

PATTIE
No, that's too old.

KIMBERLY
I like it. Keep it on, Aunt Debra.

DEBRA
(*to* PATTIE)
Kim and I have the same taste in music.

(PATTIE *sneers at* DEBRA. BUDDY *has taken a small light-box out of the bag. He goes to plug it in.*)

PATTIE
(*trying to be normal*)
How was school, Kim?

KIMBERLY
(*confused*)
What?

PATTIE
How was school?

KIMBERLY
Fine.
(*pops the Trouble bubble*)

DEBRA
(*returning to game*)
You need a six to get out of Home Base.
(*pops Trouble bubble*)
Damn. Four. Your turn, Pattie.

PATTIE
What'd you *do* at school?

KIMBERLY
We had a discussion about the Holocaust.

(PATTIE *can't pop the Pop-O-Matic bubble with her bandaged hands, so she leans over and tries to push it with her chin.*)

PATTIE
(*struggling with popper*)
Oh, the Holocaust. That's sounds very interesting. You know, some people say it didn't actually happen.

DEBRA
What people say the Holocaust didn't happen?

PATTIE
Just some people I know. Mind your own business, Debra. (*She presses the bubble.*)
Six! I'm out. Move my man, Kim. I go again.
(PATTIE *leans over and tries to press the Pop-O-Matic bubble again.*)

PATTIE
Isn't this nice? Playing games, chatting about the Holocaust. (*pops the popper*)
Two! Move me two!

(BUDDY *turns off the overhead light and clicks on the baby's light-box. Colorful animals are projected onto the walls, spinning around the room.*)

BUDDY
How about that, huh?

PATTIE
Oh, isn't that the cutest thing?

BUDDY
They're animals.

DEBRA
Oh yeah.

PATTIE
Carmelita's gonna love it.

BUDDY
Who's Carmelita?

PATTIE
Our baby. Kimberly named her.

DEBRA
It's your roll, Buddy. You're red.

KIMBERLY
I almost suggested Tashanda.

PATTIE
Oo! That can be her *middle* name! Carmelita Tashanda Levaco!

DEBRA
What the hell kinda name is that?

BUDDY
   (*pops the popper*)
I got a three.

KIMBERLY
   (*pops the popper*)
I got a five.

BUDDY
   (*pulls* KIMBERLY *to her feet*)
You know how to swing dance, honey?

KIMBERLY
I don't know.

PATTIE
Hey, I thought we were playing this game?

BUDDY
We're taking a dance break.

DEBRA
   (*pops the popper*)
You know, they have all sorts of dance clubs in Miami.

PATTIE
Miami? What do you know about Miami?

DEBRA
I know they have dance clubs and palm trees, and it's a lot nicer than New Jersey.

(BUDDY *and* KIMBERLY *kind of dance to the swing music, but not very well. The animals spin around on the walls.*)

BUDDY
(*dancing with* KIM)
Remember we would dance like this, Pattie?

PATTIE
No I do not.

BUDDY
At Kukla's Underage Club? When I was courtin' ya?

KIMBERLY
I didn't know you were courted, Mom.

PATTIE
(*pops popper*)
I got another six. Move my guy out.

(DEBRA *moves* PATTIE's *piece.* PATTIE *pops the popper again.* BUDDY *and* KIMBERLY *dance.*)

PATTIE
Now four. Move the other guy.
(DEBRA *does.*)

KIMBERLY
Were you ever courted, Aunt Debra?

DEBRA
Yeah, in a different way I was.

PATTIE
(*watches* BUDDY)
He's such a ham. Remember he played *The Music Man* in high school?

DEBRA
He was good.

PATTIE
Yeah. I always thought he was gonna be somebody.

BUDDY
Did I mention a Catholic school kid popped by my booth today? She sold me five raffle tickets. Grand prize is a family trip to the Alamo.

PATTIE
The *Alamo*? She didn't have any tickets to Hawaii?

DEBRA
I'm popping for you, Bud.
 (*she does*)
You got a two. Now you, Kim.
 (*she pops*)
You got a four.

BUDDY
You know, Davy Crocket fought at the Alamo.

KIMBERLY
Remember when Dad was Davy Crocket for Halloween?

PATTIE
Yeah, he went trick or treating three sheets to the wind and took a header off the Dooleys' porch.

BUDDY
Never did find that coonskin cap.

DEBRA
I missed this. Living under a roof like this. When I was in the woods, I could hear the coyotes sniffing at the flap of my tent. That was some scary shit.

PATTIE
Buddy, go get my tape recorder. I want the baby to know how much fun her family had.

DEBRA
Leave them alone. They're dancing.
 (*pops the popper*)
I got a six!

(*pops again*)
Another six!
(*pops again*)
And a one! And you're out, Pattie.
(*lands on* PATTIE's *piece, sends it home*)

PATTIE
You bitch.

DEBRA
Am I in *Trouble*?

PATTIE
Damn straight you're in trouble, you whore.

DEBRA
Now-now.
(KIMBERLY's *face suddenly drops. She's breathing hard. She stops dancing.*)

BUDDY
Are you okay honey?

PATTIE
Of course she is. We're having a good time here.
(KIM *is wincing in pain.*)

BUDDY
Kim?

KIMBERLY
Oww. Dad—
(KIM *grabs her chest in pain.*)

BUDDY
What's the matter?

PATTIE
You see, you had to get her worked up.

DEBRA
Is it your chest, honey?
(KIMBERLY *nods and slips to the floor.*)

BUDDY

Hold on, sweetie.

PATTIE

What's the matter with her?

BUDDY

Debra, call an ambulance.

KIMBERLY

Mom . . .

(*The colorful animals spin around the room. The music blares. Blackout.*)

Act Two

Scene One

(Lights up on BUDDY *with the tape recorder. He's somewhere outside. It's snowing.)*

BUDDY

And the thing is, I don't think I'm very good with kids. I mean I *like* kids, I just never pictured myself as a father. I'm more of a bachelor uncle type, you know? Which isn't to say I regret anything. I love Kim, and I'm happy you're coming, but . . . when you're young you imagine doin' a bunch of different things. Just . . . crazy, unrealistic stuff but . . . And then, when Pattie got pregnant with Kim, it was like "Oh, okay, I guess I do *this* then." Which was fine. Made things easier in some ways, you know, to not have any . . . choices I guess. I mean, most guys in the world are just guys who go to work, right? Guys with kids. So there's no shame in that. Just being a regular person.

(beat)

Although I would still like to travel someday. That's something I'd like to do. I'll see these countries on TV and think, "Wow, that's a weird place. I'd like to see that in person maybe." Like Pamplona. That's in Spain, and the bulls run through the streets chasing everybody, and the guys scramble up the sides of buildings and jump in doorways and some people get gored. It looks fun. I'd like that. But you need money to see things, so . . .

(pause)

Your mom and I spent a few days on the Jersey Shore once. Right after we got married. Well not *right* after, but when we saved enough. That was nice. And you know what's funny? When we decided to leave Secaucus, I was like, "All right, we're finally going somewhere." But then we came to Bogota. Which isn't really the someplace I had in mind but . . . What are ya gonna do?

(beat)
Those Alamo raffle tickets didn't work out either. It was in the paper. Some retired gardener won. Like *he* needed a vacation.
(beat)
See the world, Carmelita. That's my advice to you.
(beat)
Pattie's gonna be mad I'm using her tape recorder, but . . . I got nothin' else to do. Haven't had a drink in eight days. I promised Kim. See that? I'm a good guy. I don't know what Pattie's been saying on these things, but I'm tellin' you straight. I'm a good guy.

(Crossfade to . . .)

Scene Two

(Lights up in KIMBERLY's *bedroom.* KIM *is in her bed. Her hair has turned a shock of white. She's recovering.* PATTIE, DEBRA, *and* JEFF *are all here playing Dungeons & Dragons with* KIM. JEFF, *the Dungeon Master, has a module screen propped up in front of him. Behind the screen, he rolls a multitude of dice, reads from a module, and refers to maps. The others all have character sheets that they refer to during the game, which is heated and energetic. There are a couple of D&D books lying around.* PATTIE's *hands are still bandaged. Also, one of her legs is now in a cast.)*

JEFF
The passageway divides east or west.

KIMBERLY
West.

JEFF
You head west for twenty feet and you reach a door.

DEBRA
Gandrella, the Half-Elvin Thief, listens at the door.

JEFF
(rolls dice)
You hear nothing.

DEBRA
I check for traps.

JEFF
(*rolls dice*)
Gandrella finds no traps.

PATTIE
Weslocke draws her sword.

DEBRA
Gandrella draws her dagger.

KIMBERLY
Polenta draws her staff.

PATTIE
I open the door.

JEFF
The door opens with a creak. Beyond it is a room cluttered with mangled pieces of armor. On a pedestal in the center of the room appears to be a gold statuette in the shape of a Manticore.

PATTIE
What's a Manticore?

KIMBERLY
I'll look it up in the Monster Manual.
(*looks through one of the books*)

PATTIE
Let's go to another room.

DEBRA
No, it's a gold statue. It's treasure.

PATTIE
That's what you said at the cauldron, then those Troglodytes jumped out and pummeled us with clubs.

KIMBERLY
(*holds out Monster Manual*)
Look. That's a Manticore.

ACT TWO

PATTIE
I'm leaving.

KIMBERLY
I'm going inside.

PATTIE
Kim, what are you doing?!

KIMBERLY
Be brave, Mom.

DEBRA
I'll go with Kim.

PATTIE
Look at the book! It has claws and wings and a lion's body!

DEBRA
You have to come with us, Pattie. Weslocke is the Fighter!

KIMBERLY
We need your eighteen strength.

PATTIE
Aww, fine.

JEFF
You enter the room. The door slams shut behind you.

PATTIE
I *knew* it!

JEFF
Four Manticores swoop down from the ceiling and begin attacking you.
(*The women start screaming heatedly.*)

PATTIE	DEBRA	KIMBERLY
I hack the motherfuckers with my sword! I behead as many as I can! I knew there wasn't free treasure!	I attack with my dagger! I aim for the throat. Remember I have plus three on attacks because I have an eighteen dexterity!	I whack one really hard with my wooden staff and then jump out of the way and start chanting a spell!

JEFF
Hold on! They get the initiative because they surprised *you*.

DEBRA
Don't get excited, Kim. You're supposed to be recovering.

PATTIE
Didn't I tell you we'd get attacked?!

JEFF
(*rolling dice*)
Two of the Manticores go for Gandrella and two for Weslocke.

DEBRA
What about Polenta?

JEFF
They ignore Kim for now.

PATTIE
You're playing favorites!

JEFF
It's all in the dice, ladies. Live with it.

PATTIE
How much hit point damage?

JEFF
(*rolling dice*)
Let's see . . . claws, teeth, spikes . . . That's twenty-nine for Gandrella. And . . . forty-three for Weslocke.

PATTIE
Aw, gimme a fucking break!

JEFF
Mrs. Levaco, please.

PATTIE
I'm negative eleven!

DEBRA
I'm negative nine.

JEFF
You're both dead.

PATTIE

This game sucks!

DEBRA

Can Polenta resurrect us with magic?

JEFF

Kim, you're surrounded by Manticores. What are you gonna do?

KIMBERLY
(*looking at her list of spells*)
I cast a . . . Teleport spell, so we're transported back to that magic fountain of healing.

JEFF
(*rolls dice, pause*)
Before the incantation is out of your mouth, the Manticores descend upon you. One tears off your arm, another digs its claws into your back. Iron spikes shoot into you from all sides. Another rips your throat out. Essentially you're torn to shreds.

DEBRA
(*beat*)
Is she dead?

JEFF

Yeah.

PATTIE

Is this supposed to be a kids' game? This is *sick*.

KIMBERLY

They tore out my throat? Cool.

DEBRA

That's it? We've been playing this stupid game for three and a half days and just like that we're all dead?!

JEFF

It was very careless of you to jump into the room like that.

DEBRA

Well, do over.

JEFF

I'm afraid I can't do that.

DEBRA
This is bull-shit!

JEFF
A valiant attempt on your noble journey. But the gods were not with our adventurers today.

DEBRA
This kid's a geek.

KIMBERLY
We thank you Dungeon Master for your time and patience.

JEFF
Not a problem, wise and decomposing sage.

KIMBERLY
That was fun.

PATTIE
(*suddenly*)
Oh my gosh, it's time for my pills. Kim, it's time for your pills too. Isn't this fun? We all take pills.

DEBRA
I don't take no pills.

JEFF
I'm on Ritalin.

PATTIE
Ooo, Ritalin. Can I try one of those?

JEFF
I'm not really allowed to hand them out.

PATTIE
Fuck ya then. Greedy prick.

KIMBERLY
Mom . . .

PATTIE
(*grabs crutches and pulls herself up*)
I-know-I-know, nickels in the jar.

JEFF
I never asked. What happened to your leg, Mrs. Levaco?

PATTIE
When Kim was staying at the hospital with her heart attack, I snuck out back for a quick smoke and I fell off the loading dock.

JEFF
Oh. You probably shouldn't have been smoking anyway.

PATTIE
Hey, I smoked when I was pregnant with Kim and nothin' happened to *her*!

(PATTIE *exits.*)

JEFF
I'd like to put your Mom in a room with my Dad and conduct experiments.

DEBRA
How you feeling, Kim?

KIMBERLY
Good.

DEBRA
Doing your exercises? Eating right?

KIMBERLY
Uh-huh.

JEFF
She goes back to school tomorrow.

DEBRA
Is that right?

KIMBERLY
Dad says I can.

DEBRA
That's great. I'm real proud of you. Fightin' back, stayin' strong. Get back up on that horse, right?

KIMBERLY
I guess.

DEBRA
That's terrific. So . . . maybe we can go back to our plan then?

KIMBERLY
Yeah, I'd like that. How 'bout we do it tomorrow? Right after school.

DEBRA
Hey, wow, all right. That's what I like. Raring to go.

JEFF
I think it's too soon, though. If Kim—

DEBRA
She said she was okay.

JEFF
I know, but she's supposed to rest. What's a couple days?

KIMBERLY
In Kimberly Time, it's about a week and a half. It's like dog years.

DEBRA
(*amused*)
Dog years, that's good.

KIMBERLY
You said we get half the money, right?

DEBRA
Right. Just like we said.

KIMBERLY
Because I was thinking maybe that wasn't so fair.

DEBRA
(*beat*)
What do you mean?

KIMBERLY
Me and Jeff having to split half, and you getting the whole other half to yourself. That's a little wonky.

DEBRA
Wonky? It's *my* idea.

KIMBERLY
But *we're* doing all the work.

DEBRA
Work?! I dragged a mailbox eight blocks in the dead of night!

KIMBERLY
I think it should be an even split. Three ways.

DEBRA
What are you talkin' about? This ain't a friggen hoagie we're cuttin' up.

KIMBERLY
But you can't do it without us. I just think an even split would be more fair.

DEBRA
Did you talk her into this?

JEFF
No, I didn't say anything.

KIMBERLY
You wanna do it or not?

DEBRA
What's going on, Kim? You don't need money.

KIMBERLY
Yes I do.

DEBRA
For what?

KIMBERLY
For family stuff.

DEBRA
What family stuff?

KIMBERLY
None of your business. I didn't ask you what you were gonna do with your money.

DEBRA
I told you, I'm going to Miami.

KIMBERLY
Good for you. One third of the money is plenty to get there. So we'll go to the bank after school then?

DEBRA
I don't frickin' believe this. You're rolling me.

KIMBERLY
What's fair is fair, Aunt Debra. Don't you wanna be fair?

DEBRA
Screw you, Kim. You play this injured little twerp and— You're *hustling* me.

KIMBERLY
Fine then, forget it. It's off.

DEBRA
Kim—!

KIMBERLY
No, Jeff's right, I'm not one hundred percent.
(*feigns faintness, lies down*)

DEBRA
Jesus! Fine! Three-way split! Goddamnit.

KIMBERLY
(*sits back up*)
So we'll meet at the library tomorrow, get ready and head over to the bank.
(*to* JEFF)
You okay with that?

JEFF
I guess.

KIMBERLY
All right then.

DEBRA
A shakedown. My own flesh and blood. That's rotten.
(PATTIE *enters with pill bottles.*)

PATTIE
Can someone help me open these? I just cracked a tooth.
(*Blackout.*)

Scene Three

(*Lights up in the kitchen. The jar on the table is now overflowing with nickels.* BUDDY, *in his chef's hat, sets up cereal bowls and Bran Flakes for breakfast.* KIMBERLY *comes in, markedly slower.*)

BUDDY
The kid is up and about. Look at her go. So excited to get back to school. The anxious scholar. Racing to the breakfast table.

KIMBERLY
Don't be a dick, Dad.

BUDDY
We've got a healthy breakfast. Startin' the day off right.

KIMBERLY
Where's the Cap'n Crunch?

BUDDY
Doctor Cavanaugh said fiber-fiber-fiber.

KIMBERLY
But I'm better now. Can't we switch back?

BUDDY
Here's some milk. You also need calcium, he said. We don't want you breaking a hip.

KIMBERLY
I don't want any milk.

BUDDY
If I can drink it, *you* can drink it.
(*He holds his glass of milk up.* KIMBERLY, *sitting, holds hers up. They both drink the milk.*)

BUDDY
How you feeling?

KIMBERLY
How *you* feeling?

BUDDY
I feel great.

KIMBERLY
Me too. You look well-rested.

BUDDY
Thank you. It's the calcium.

KIMBERLY
Uh-huh.
 (*notices a book on the table*)
What is this?

BUDDY
Oh, I uh—

KIMBERLY
A Bible?

BUDDY
I know we've never been religious people, but I thought you might wanna take a look at—

KIMBERLY
Is this because we played D and D?

BUDDY
I'm trying to give you your space, Kim. If you wanna play that game, that's your choice, but I wanna present an alternative to—

KIMBERLY
Geez Dad, let it go.

BUDDY
Your mother said you were all murdered by winged demons.

KIMBERLY
They weren't demons. They were Manticores.

BUDDY

I was flipping through Leviticus this morning. Some of it's pretty racy. You might like it.

(KIMBERLY *eats her cereal.*)

BUDDY

You know, we used to go to church when you were a baby. Your mom played the organ.

(PATTIE *enters in a nightgown. She's still on her crutches.*)

PATTIE

Morning.

BUDDY

Hey Pattie, remember you used to play the organ? If those bandages come off soon, maybe you can get back to that.

PATTIE

Forget the organ, I'll be happy when I can wipe my own ass.

BUDDY

(*beat*)
Yeah, me too.

(PATTIE *has crossed to the bathroom.*)

KIMBERLY

(*looks up at the clock, then asks . . .*)
Was Aunt Debra up yet?

BUDDY

No. She sleeps to noon every day. Why would she be up?

KIMBERLY

I don't know. I thought she said something about going for a jog.

BUDDY

A jog? Debra?

KIMBERLY

I don't know. Maybe I misheard her.

BUDDY

(*pause*)
Kim, I don't want you spending too much time with her.

KIMBERLY
Aunt Debra?

BUDDY
She's got a lot of problems.

KIMBERLY
Compared to who?

BUDDY
Just do me a favor and don't get involved in any of her shenanigans.

KIMBERLY
Shenanigans? Nice word, Dad.

BUDDY
(calls to PATTIE*)*
Your daughter's making fun of me.

PATTIE
(off)
Don't do that, Kim. Your father's sensitive.

BUDDY
How's your friend by the way?

KIMBERLY
My friend?

BUDDY
Yeah, the kid. From Zippy Burger.

KIMBERLY
Jeff?

BUDDY
Yeah. How's Jeff?

KIMBERLY
He's fine.

BUDDY
Good.
(pause)
So you like that boy?

KIMBERLY
Dad—

BUDDY
I know, I handled it all wrong in the car, but I'm your father so— And I'm sure he's a nice kid but . . . you like him?

KIMBERLY
Yeah, Dad. What are you—

BUDDY
I just don't know him at all, so I wanna ask questions, make sure he has only good intentions.

KIMBERLY
What are you worried about? I went through menopause four years ago.

BUDDY
Aw geez, Kim—

KIMBERLY
He's not gonna get me pregnant.

BUDDY
Come on, that's not what I—

PATTIE
(*off*)
Buddy, I'm finished! Come wipe me!

BUDDY
I'll be right back.

(BUDDY *runs into the bathroom.* KIMBERLY *eats her cereal.* DEBRA *enters in a nightgown, exhausted. She carries a dufflebag.*)

DEBRA
Where's the coffee?

KIMBERLY
It's about time. You said you'd be up.

DEBRA
I *am* up.

KIMBERLY
You're late. Did you get my stuff?

DEBRA
It's right here.
(hands her dufflebag)

KIMBERLY
Where'd you get it?

DEBRA
(pours herself some coffee)
Salvation Army. They've got a nice selection.

KIMBERLY
(opens bag and looks inside)
God, it's ugly.

DEBRA
It's supposed to be ugly, now put it away. Save it for later.

KIMBERLY
(puts dress back, zips bag)
Jeff wanted to know if he needed to wear anything special.

DEBRA
What's he mean special? He's playing himself. There's nothing to— If that kid messes this up—
(sound of toilet flushing)

DEBRA
All right, keep quiet about it.
(BUDDY *re-enters.*)

BUDDY
That was a lovely way to start the day.
(sees DEBRA, *looks up at clock, then back at her)*
Got some plans for the day?

DEBRA
What, I can't get up early?

BUDDY
What's in the dufflebag?

KIMBERLY

That's mine. School project.

BUDDY

Huh. Awful lot of school projects.

(*Sound of the electric toothbrush whirring.* BUDDY *prepares a bowl of cereal for* PATTIE.)

BUDDY

(*to* DEBRA)
You *could* look for a job today. Earn some money to pay me back for that stereo.

DEBRA

Again with that stereo. It's too early, Buddy. And the fact is, you owed it to me. So shut up about it.

BUDDY

What *owed* you?

DEBRA

You agreed to give it to me.

BUDDY

Agreed? I didn't agree to—
(*stops himself*)
You know what? Forget it.

DEBRA

No, you've been forgetting it all week. You throw out these little digs and then retreat back to your corner and it's starting to tick me off.

BUDDY

It's a good day, Debra, don't go pissing on it.

DEBRA

Who brought up the stereo? Was it me? Did I bring up the stereo, Kim?

BUDDY

(*calls off*)
What kind of cereal you want, Pattie?

                    PATTIE
(*off*)
Whatever, so long as you put the berries on!

                    DEBRA
You've obviously got something on your mind. You got something on your mind?

                    BUDDY
No.

                    DEBRA
Whaddaya wanna know, Buddy?

                    BUDDY
Nothin'. I know more than enough. I don't wanna know anymore. You'll implicate me.

                    DEBRA
Implicate you? You're implicated already. I wasn't the one who—

                    BUDDY
I don't wanna talk about this, Debra.

                    DEBRA
Then why do you keep bringing up that piece of junk stereo?

                    BUDDY
It wasn't a piece of junk! It was vintage!

                    DEBRA
Did you or did you not agree to give it to me?

                    BUDDY
Yeah, I did, if you did what you said you would do, which you didn't.

                    DEBRA
I tried to.

                    BUDDY
But you *didn't*. *Trying* isn't *doing*.

                    DEBRA
But I went to *do* it. It's not my fault it *didn't happen*.

BUDDY
(*notices* KIM's *listening*)
All right, drop it.

KIMBERLY
Don't drop it on my account.

(PATTIE *re-enters.*)

PATTIE
I love that electric toothbrush.

DEBRA
We had an agreement.

BUDDY
The agreement—block your ears, Kim—the agreement was I'd give you the stereo if you went next door and slapped the guy around.

KIMBERLY
What guy?

PATTIE
Mr. Hicks.

BUDDY
Which you did not do.

KIMBERLY
You hired Aunt Debra to beat up Mr. Hicks?

PATTIE
My gums feels so clean.

KIMBERLY
Why would you do that?

BUDDY
Because of his goddamn cabbages. They kept spreading into our yard, and I told him to cut them back. How many times did I tell him, Pattie?

PATTIE
Many times.

BUDDY
And he would just wave his hand, like *I* was the crazy one.

KIMBERLY
So why didn't you beat him up yourself?

BUDDY
He was my neighbor. I can't beat up my own neighbor.

KIMBERLY
You people are freaks.

PATTIE
I had nothing to do with this episode.

DEBRA
You did so. Come on, Pattie, you know damn well what—

BUDDY
Mrs. Denton said she saw a masked intruder crawl in his window. Did you wear a mask?

DEBRA
Yes. A pig mask.

BUDDY
A pig mask? What the hell's the matter with you?

DEBRA
I didn't wanna be identified. You told me to scare him.

BUDDY
I didn't tell you to *kill* him.

DEBRA
I didn't know he had a weak heart. I didn't even do anything. He just took one look at me and dropped dead.

BUDDY
You were wearing a pig mask! If a pig-lady crawled in my window, I'd drop dead too!

KIMBERLY
That's why we left Secaucus? Because you killed Mr. Hicks?

DEBRA
Nobody killed anybody.

ACT TWO

BUDDY
Kim, go wait in the car.

DEBRA
The guy just died.

KIMBERLY
With a little help.

PATTIE
He was very old, honey.

DEBRA
I didn't even touch him. It wouldn't hold up in court, I'll tell ya that much.

BUDDY
He shoulda cut those cabbages back like I told him.

DEBRA
It wasn't just cabbages, Buddy—

KIMBERLY
This is so wrong. Don't you even feel bad?
(They all consider this for a couple beats. Then a little too late they say:)

BUDDY   DEBRA   PATTIE
Of course I feel bad.   I feel just terrible.   An awful way to go.

KIMBERLY
I'll be in the car.

BUDDY
Now don't go telling your friends about this, Kim. It's family business. Keep it that way.
(KIM grabs the keys from the hook and exits with the dufflebag.)

BUDDY
Why'd you say anything in front of her?

DEBRA
You brought it up.

BUDDY
Jesus, Debra—

DEBRA
Hey, none of it woulda happened if Pattie hadn't done what she did, so don't go blaming me, Buddy!

PATTIE
Debra, I'm pregnant and easily upset, so don't start in on me!

BUDDY
All right, now calm down—

DEBRA
If I hear another fuckin' word about that stereo—!

BUDDY
All right, forget it! You got the stereo, that's it! I'm sorry I ever brought the damn thing up!

DEBRA
I can't wait to get away from you goddamn animals!
(*storms off and slams a door*)

BUDDY
(*rummaging in his pocket for nickels*)
Who let her in the house? I never invited her back in.
(*pulls out handful of nickels*)
I lost count of the— I don't even know how much we owe here.

(BUDDY *adds a few nickels to the pile, then picks up* PATTIE's *cereal bowl and feeds her with a spoon.*)

PATTIE
They don't care about me. Neither of them. I'm pregnant, and my leg's broken, I have carpal tunnel and cancer.

BUDDY
You don't have cancer.

PATTIE
Yes I do, plus diabetes and a chipped tooth.

BUDDY
Come on, relax.
(*holds out spoon*)
Take a bite.

PATTIE
(*mouth-full*)
And I do feel bad about Mr. Hicks. He was very sweet.

BUDDY
I know.

PATTIE
I'm gonna miss him.

BUDDY
All right.

PATTIE
More berries.
(*He scoops more berries onto her cereal.*)

BUDDY
She was so upset.

PATTIE
She was born upset.
(*They lock eyes.*)

PATTIE
What?

BUDDY
It's our fault, isn't it?

PATTIE
Mr. Hicks?

BUDDY
Kimberly. You put our genes together and it comes out poison.

PATTIE
Kim isn't poison.

BUDDY
That's not what I meant.

PATTIE
I know what ya meant, Buddy, and I don't wanna hear it. She's sixteen, we're not gonna start blaming people now. Things get passed on all the time. I got my mother's ass. You think I blame my mother for my ass?

BUDDY
It's not the same, Pattie.

PATTIE
Can you stop? Please?
(*She takes another bite of cereal, chews, and swallows.*)

PATTIE
You're a lot more bearable when you're on the sauce, ya know it?
(*Lights crossfade to . . .*)

Scene Four

(*The library.* DEBRA *and* JEFF *are waiting for* KIM. JEFF, *with a pad and pencil, has been working on another anagram.*)

JEFF
Debra Watts, right? And Watts is W-A-T-T-S?

DEBRA
Uh-huh.

JEFF
(*small talk while working on anagram*)
You ever been in re-hab?

DEBRA
None of your business.

JEFF
'Cause my brother's in rehab, and my Dad visits him like every day. But me, the old guy barely speaks to. Can you explain that to me?

DEBRA
No, I can't.

JEFF
I think he just likes screw-ups, that's what I think. Hey, maybe if we get caught and thrown in jail, he'll come visit me, and then he'll *have* to talk to me.

DEBRA

Listen, you little whine-bag, if you get caught, nobody's coming to visit you because you'll be in the morgue with my shoe up your ass.

JEFF

(*puts down pencil*)
Finished. For Debra Watts, I've come up with Basted Wart, Wasted Brat, and Wet Bastard.

DEBRA

Thanks. Those are cute. Where's Kim?

JEFF

In the bathroom.

DEBRA

Taking her time, ain't she? What is she *doing* anyway?

JEFF

Just getting changed.

DEBRA

I mean later. With the money. Why'd she suddenly want more money?

JEFF

She just thought you should be fair.

DEBRA

Come on, is she buying something?

JEFF

I don't know.

DEBRA

I hope you lie better than that at the bank.

JEFF

Really, she didn't—

DEBRA

Because they are gonna see right through you. Those tellers are tricky. Very perceptive.
  (*looks up at the clock*)
What is taking her so long?

JEFF

Can I ask you something?

DEBRA

Do you have to?

JEFF

How much longer is she gonna live?

DEBRA

(*pause*)
Why you asking me? How am I supposed to know something like—

JEFF

Because I wrote a paper, and everything said the life expectancy is sixteen. And Kim's *already* sixteen, so—

DEBRA

Look, I don't know. You asked me a question, and I don't know the answer, so drop it.

JEFF

(*pause*)
You think Carmelita will be like her?

DEBRA

No chance.

JEFF

Why no chance? Kim said the Levacos always have a one in four chance of—

DEBRA

It's a non-issue, kid. Don't sweat it. The baby'll be fine.
(KIM *enters dressed in old-lady clothes. She has the make-up of an old lady, and an old lady hat and purse. The transformation is stunning. No one can speak for a couple beats.*)

DEBRA

Jesus.

KIMBERLY

It's okay?

DEBRA
You look like Rose Kennedy.

KIMBERLY
It's okay, though?

DEBRA
It's perfect. God. I had no idea it'd be so . . . you look so *old*.

KIMBERLY
So it'll work then?

DEBRA
Yeah. If the kid can keep a straight face, we're golden.

KIMBERLY
(*to* JEFF)
I look okay?
(JEFF *looks at her, ill at ease.*)

DEBRA
It's not a beauty contest.

KIMBERLY
It's just for a little while.

JEFF
I know. Yeah, it looks good.

DEBRA
All right, you gotta get over there before they close. You wanna run through it once.

KIMBERLY
I think we got it.

DEBRA
And you got the checks?

JEFF
Right here.

DEBRA
And the dufflebag? Keep the money in the dufflebag.

KIMBERLY
Got it.

DEBRA
Okay then. Now I don't wanna be spotted on the camera, so I'm gonna wait here. You come right back afterwards. I'll be waiting.

KIMBERLY
Just one final thing, though.

DEBRA
What?

KIMBERLY
Why is Carmelita a non-issue?

DEBRA
(*pause*)
Carmelita?

KIMBERLY
You just told Jeff there was no chance of her being like me.

DEBRA
You heard that?

KIMBERLY
How is it a non-issue?

DEBRA
Kim, the bank closes at four, so—

KIMBERLY
It's because of Mr. Hicks, right?

DEBRA
Hey, I'm not supposed to—

KIMBERLY
That's why my father wanted you to slap him around, right? It wasn't just the cabbages.

DEBRA
You gotta understand, your mother's baby-crazy. It's all she ever wanted. Even as a kid. You should've seen her with the dolls.

KIMBERLY
I knew it didn't make sense.

DEBRA
She was miserable in Secaucus. You should be glad she has something that makes her happy. I said, "Pattie, if you're so miserable, do something about it."

KIMBERLY
You told her to do it?

DEBRA
I didn't tell her to screw Hicks! I just said— She had options. She could've adopted. Or kidnaped. Or . . . I know a guy who sells 'em. You all don't have that kinda money, but I bet he'd work some sort of barter system. He's a friend of mine.

KIMBERLY
(to JEFF*)*
You ready?

JEFF
Yeah.

DEBRA
When Cinnamon died, I bought you a gerbil, right? Same difference, Kim, so don't start pulling an attitude.

KIMBERLY
Same difference?

DEBRA
Well, maybe not technically, but it's the same idea.

KIMBERLY
Okay, Aunt Debra. You're gonna wait here, right?

DEBRA
Right.

KIMBERLY
(to JEFF*)*
Let's go.

DEBRA
Don't say I said anything. Your dad's real sensitive about it.

KIMBERLY
We'll be back.
(KIM *and* JEFF *head for the exit. It takes* KIM *a while to get there.*)

DEBRA
(*trying to make light*)
Hey, you better step livelier than that. I'd like to be in Miami sometime this century.
(*beat*)
The tortoise doesn't always win the race, you know.
(KIM *keeps walking.*)
Kidding.
(*beat*)
You know I'm kidding, right? Beautiful?
(*no response*)
I'll be waiting.
(KIMBERLY *and* JEFF *exit. Lights fade on* DEBRA.)

Scene Five

(*Lights up in the kitchen. There are now two overflowing jars of nickels on the table.* BUDDY *and* PATTIE *are walking around.* PATTIE, *between contractions, isn't really in pain at the moment.*)

BUDDY
Just keep moving. There you go.

PATTIE
How long's it been?

BUDDY
Fifteen minutes.

PATTIE
I'm scared, Buddy. I think we should go.

BUDDY

They said not until they're five to seven minutes apart. This could go on. You wanna wait around a hospital for six hours?

PATTIE

No. Too many germs.

BUDDY

All right then. It's a quick drive. We're fine.

PATTIE

Well then distract me. You're supposed to distract me! Did you pick up the paint swatches?

BUDDY

Yeah, right here.
 (*hands her a paint swatch*)

PATTIE

What's this?

BUDDY

It's slate. Everything matches slate.

PATTIE

That's all they had?

BUDDY

That's all they had on sale.

PATTIE

Who cares about sales?! It's a *baby's* room! Mrs. Gigante says Bonnie's room is pink! Why didn't you bring me any pink swatches?

BUDDY

The pink wasn't on sale.

PATTIE

If you had half a brain, you'd be dangerous.
 (KIMBERLY *enters with the dufflebag and crosses to her room.*)

PATTIE

Oh hi, honey. I'm in labor.

BUDDY

Where were you?

KIMBERLY

(*crossing to bedroom*)
At the bank.

BUDDY

What were you doing at the bank?

KIMBERLY

(*exits into her bedroom*)
Nothing.

PATTIE

(*beat*)
What is she wearing?

BUDDY

I don't know.

PATTIE

(*calls off*)
Was there a costume party at school, honey?
(*to* BUDDY)
She likes when we ask her about school.

BUDDY

Why are you wearing those clothes?

KIMBERLY

(*off*)
I'm trying a new style.

PATTIE

(*to* BUDDY)
That's how teens are. Remember senior year? You walked around in that pirate hat?

BUDDY

Two days. That's all I wore it. Don't start in on me.

PATTIE

(*getting a contraction*)
Uh-oh. Uh-oh! Here it comes again.

BUDDY
(*timing her*)
Okay . . .

PATTIE
ow-ow-ow-Ow-OW-OW!

BUDDY
Breathe through it.

PATTIE
Slate! I can't believe you bring home *slate*!

BUDDY
Focus, Pattie.

PATTIE
They paint *prisons* slate!

BUDDY
Keep breathing.

PATTIE
I ask you to do *one* thing! Get a couple swatches and—OW, Mother of God!

BUDDY
(*looking at watch*)
It should be coming down now.

PATTIE
(*the pain fades*)
Okay . . . okay . . . okay . . .

BUDDY
There you go. Aaaand . . . walk it off.

PATTIE
(*The contraction has passed.*)
Walk it off? I didn't twist an ankle! It's a fucking contraction! Walk it off, he says, like I'm in Little League. You think I'm in Little League, ya asshole?!

BUDDY
(*sighs, takes her in*)
No, I don't think you're in Little League.

(*He tosses a couple more nickels onto the pile, then moves to the fridge.*)

PATTIE

Where are you going?

BUDDY

I'm getting a beer.

PATTIE

Oo, get me one, too.

BUDDY

Pattie . . .

PATTIE

It'll soothe me!
(*makes her way to a seat*)
Hey Kimmy, did you hear my contraction?

KIMBERLY

(*off*)
Yeah, it set off the Gigantes' car alarm.

PATTIE

What can I say? My voice carries.
(*beat*)
Did ya notice the snow started melting today? I take that as a good omen. Whaddaya think?

BUDDY

(*hands her beer*)
Sure. Whatever.

PATTIE

(*gently*)
I think the room should be pink, Buddy. It's important to me. I want it to be perfect.

BUDDY

(*pause*)
I know you do.
(*Beat.* PATTIE *swigs her beer.*)

PATTIE
(*calls off*)
Hey Kim, your Dad and I were talking, and when your sister comes, you're gonna have to sleep on the couch for a little while. You don't mind, do you?
(KIMBERLY *re-enters in her regular clothes.*)

PATTIE
Oh, nice of you to make an appearance.

KIMBERLY
Why do I have to sleep on the couch?

PATTIE
Because the baby needs her own room.

KIMBERLY
Why?

PATTIE
Because she does. It's important. For the development. It helps them be independent.

BUDDY
I can sleep on the couch, if you'd rather sleep with Mom.

KIMBERLY
Why can't the baby sleep with Mom?

PATTIE
Because babies cry. And I need my sleep.
(KIMBERLY *notices Buddy's beer.*)

BUDDY
(*off her look*)
It's one beer, Kimmy. I'm under a lot of pressure at the moment.
(KIM *goes back into her room.*)

BUDDY
I have been very good! It's not easy, you know!
(*under his breath*)
Goddamnit.

PATTIE
They say a new sibling can be hard on the first-born.

BUDDY
Maybe she can share the room.

PATTIE
She doesn't need to. That's a very comfortable couch.
(calls off)
You were conceived on that couch!

BUDDY
Don't tell her that. For godsakes, Pattie—

KIMBERLY
(off)
Was Carmelita?

PATTIE
Was Carmelita what?

KIMBERLY
(off)
Conceived on that couch?

PATTIE
That is none of your business.
(to BUDDY)
You hear this sass? She gets that from you.

KIMBERLY
(enters with a suitcase and the dufflebag)
Because she was conceived in Mr. Hicks' basement?

BUDDY
Kim—!
(SPLASH!)

PATTIE
Goddamnit. My water broke.

BUDDY
(to KIM)
What'd Aunt Debra say to you?!

ACT TWO

KIMBERLY
You tell *me*.

PATTIE
I'm soaked! You see what she did!

KIMBERLY
Is it true?

PATTIE
Get me some towels, Buddy!

KIMBERLY
Is it?

BUDDY
Kim, we're a little busy at the moment.
  (*searches for towels*)

KIMBERLY
Aunt Debra said the baby's a non-issue.

PATTIE
Aunt Debra's a psychopath.

BUDDY
Non-issue? What's that mean?

KIMBERLY
It means she won't be like me.

PATTIE
I don't even know what you're talking about.

BUDDY
Didn't I tell you to stay away from Debra?!
  (*to* PATTIE)
That is *your* sister! *You* let her back in here!

KIMBERLY
Is that why Mr. Hicks kept visiting? You didn't like Dad's odds?

BUDDY
  (*to* PATTIE)
You see?! Didn't I tell you this was gonna happen?

PATTIE
Mr. Hicks brought me cabbages. That's all! Now go to your room!

KIMBERLY
Oh, is it my room again? I thought I'd been evicted.

BUDDY
This is a very complicated issue that doesn't involve you.
    (BUDDY *runs over to* PATTIE *with a roll of paper towels.*)

PATTIE
Not *paper* towels! *Real* towels! This isn't Kool-Aid, you moron!
    (BUDDY *searches for real towels.*)

KIMBERLY
Shouldn't Mr. Hicks be doing that?

PATTIE
Now you know darn well Mr. Hicks is dead.

BUDDY
Kim, you are walking on thin ice here.

PATTIE
And even if he *wasn't* dead, he'd hardly have the stamina to run around looking for towels. He was very frail.

BUDDY
Hicks was just a neighbor; now drop it. He meant nothing to us.

KIMBERLY
Then why did you hire Aunt Debra to kill him?

BUDDY
I didn't hire her to *kill* him! Come on—
    (*brings towels to* PATTIE)
The agreement was beat him up. I was very upset at the time. But I never wanted the guy killed.

KIMBERLY
And yet he died.

BUDDY

Okay, you wanna talk about this, we'll talk about it. Later. But right now your mother's having a baby. And that's a little more important than your hissy fit!

KIMBERLY

Of course it is.

BUDDY

You're timing is *way* off.

KIMBERLY

That's the understatement of the century.

PATTIE

Don't get smart with your father.

KIMBERLY

Oh, I'm sorry to get smart. And I'm sorry my timing is off. And I'm sorry I'm not Bonnie Gigante.

PATTIE

What does *she* have to do with anything?

KIMBERLY

But for the record, Bonnie Gigante sells pot and doles out blowjobs like they were handshakes.

PATTIE

That is filthy talk! I don't know where you get that sewer-mouth.

BUDDY

Kim, I don't know what this is about, but you're being naïve and spiteful, and you need to toughen up.

KIMBERLY

Toughen up?

PATTIE

None of this is gonna matter anyway. You're gonna have a beautiful baby sister. Who cares how we got her?

KIMBERLY

I do!

BUDDY
Too bad! It's none of your business!

KIMBERLY
I can't believe you bought into this.

BUDDY
Hey—

KIMBERLY
Did you *ever* have a backbone?

PATTIE
That is your father you're talking to.

KIMBERLY
Are you sure?! One never knows in this house!

PATTIE
You apologize!

KIMBERLY
(*to* BUDDY)
You're the one who needs to toughen up!

PATTIE
Okay, yes it happened! All right?! So what?! It was a thing that was done! That's all it was! It served a purpose! Can we let it go now?!
(*silence*)
You know what, Kim? You win. We're not perfect. Okay? And we have been trying our damndest to make you happy, but we obviously can't be whatever it is you want us to be.

KIMBERLY
Well, that makes it unanimous then.

PATTIE
This has nothing to do with you. I wanted a baby. It's that simple.

KIMBERLY
You *had* a baby.

PATTIE
I wanted another baby.

KIMBERLY
You wanted a *different* baby.

BUDDY
Kim—!

KIMBERLY
And you made real sure she'd be nothing like me.

PATTIE
What choice did I have?! Soon I won't be able to have babies anymore, and then you'll die and I'll be alone! And I didn't want to be alone!
(*beat*)
I meant, *I'll* die. I was making a sister for you, so you would have someone to talk to when I died. Not you!

BUDDY
All right Pattie, relax.

PATTIE
(*notices* KIM's *suitcase*)
What's that? My suitcase for the hospital?

KIMBERLY
No. I'm staying at a friend's house.
(BUDDY *grabs a towel and wipes* PATTIE's *forehead.*)

BUDDY
What friend? You didn't ask if you could— It better not be that boy's house. His family's a mess, and I don't want you staying in that environment.

PATTIE
Help me, Buddy. It's getting hot in here.
(BUDDY *fans* PATTIE.)

KIMBERLY
You know what I wanted to do? What I was *gonna* do? With the money?

BUDDY
What money?

KIMBERLY
I wanted to walk in and say, "Hey, guess what? We're going to the Alamo!"

PATTIE
The Alamo?

KIMBERLY
Or Pamplona. Or Hawaii. One of those places Dad is always talking about. And I wanted to say, "Pack a bag, we're going right now!" And you'd be confused, but I'd explain it, and you'd be really happy, and you'd jump up and start packing. But then . . . Debra and Hicks, and I come home, and then you with the room—

PATTIE
I can't understand a word she's saying.

KIMBERLY
And I'm thinking, "Why bother?" You did a good job *pretending* for a little while, I guess, but really you gave up a long time ago.

PATTIE
Gave up *what?*

KIMBERLY
A whole mess of stuff. I can't even— It's like you're just sitting around *waiting* or something. And I know it's hard for you, and you have to prepare and cope and whatever, but . . .

BUDDY
But what?

KIMBERLY
I'm not dead yet!
   (*beat*)
I'm not dead.
   (*Silence. Then* PATTIE *gets another contraction.*)

PATTIE
Oh-oh-oh-ow-ow-Ow-OW . . . here's another one!

BUDDY
Nobody thinks you're dead.

PATTIE

(*in pain*)
What's this, Bud?! How long since the last one?

BUDDY

(*looking at watch*)
I'm not sure. Fourteen minutes maybe?

PATTIE

It hurts.

BUDDY

Do the breathing.

PATTIE

Get my suitcase. And my special pillow.

BUDDY

Okay.

(BUDDY *turns around and catches* KIM *taking the car keys off the hook. A moment passes between them. They say nothing. She puts the keys in her pocket, and he doesn't stop her.* PATTIE *talks over this exchange, unaware that it's even happening.*)

PATTIE

Also my search-a-words. I'll need something to occupy my time. And the camera. And my bathrobe, I forgot to pack my bathrobe. Plus the lip balm in my purse. Actually, just grab the whole purse.
(*turns around*)
Are you listening to me?

BUDDY

Yeah. Suitcase, pillow, search-a-words, camera . . .

PATTIE

Bathrobe and purse.

BUDDY

Bathrobe and purse.
(*exits into bedroom*)

PATTIE

Hurry up, Buddy!
(*huffing and puffing*)
It's two weeks early.

BUDDY

(*off*)
That's all right. Babies come early sometimes.

PATTIE

Kim came early. Remember? Almost did me in.
(KIM *slips out the front door with her suitcase.*)

PATTIE

(*the pain subsides*)
Oh there it goes. I think it's fading.
(*breathes easier*)
You know what Mrs. Gigante said to me this morning? She said, "Pattie, you oughtta get out and get some sun. You look like a ghost." Well, I thought, if I spent all the money she spends at that tanning salon, I'd look all brown and crunchy too. Only I didn't say that. I just said, "There's been some unseasonable weather as of late." But maybe that Alamo thing ain't such a bad idea. It's awful sunny in Texas, right, Kimmy? We'll have to buy the baby a car seat, but that can't cost so much. You think that crap-heap of a car can make it to Texas, Buddy?
(*beat*)
Kim honey, wipe my brow.
(*reaches back for her, but* KIM *isn't there*)
Kim? Where'd she go?
(DEBRA *enters the house, harried and out of breath.*)

DEBRA

Where's Kim?

PATTIE

I don't know.

DEBRA

Was she here?!

PATTIE

The baby's coming, Debra!

DEBRA

She was supposed to meet me with the money!

PATTIE

What money?
(BUDDY *re-enters with stuff for the hospital.*)

BUDDY

I'm gonna call a cab.

PATTIE

Cab? Why would we take a—
(*huge contraction*)
Owwwwwwwww!
(*Blackout.*)

Scene Six

(*Lights up on* KIM *and* JEFF *in the car.* JEFF *drives.*)

KIMBERLY

Where are we now?

JEFF

Check the map.

KIMBERLY

It says "The Wilds of Africa."

JEFF
(*He sees something run by.*)
Whoa! Did you see that gazelle?

KIMBERLY
(*reads from Safari guide*)
"In this section of the Six Flags Wild Safari, you will notice a variety of exotic and rare birds, from the common guinea fowl to our storks and cranes."

JEFF

What's that? An antelope?

KIMBERLY
(*refers to her Safari guide*)
That's a . . . I believe it's a Bontebok . . .
(*reading from the guide*)
"Characterized by its long face and horns that twist backwards, this endangered species is difficult to breed in captivity, but seems to do well in a free-roaming environment."

JEFF
I wonder if my Dad misses me.

KIMBERLY
We've only been gone two hours.

JEFF
Still, I wonder if he does.

KIMBERLY
(*pulls out tape recorder and presses Record*)
Hey Carmelita, this Safari place is unreal.

JEFF
Your mom's gonna be pissed you stole that.

KIMBERLY
We've seen black bears and camels, and now we're in Africa. You gotta see this place, only don't wait for Dad to bring you because it'll never happen.
(*hits Stop*)
This way she'll know.
(*Sound of an animal on top of the car.*)

KIMBERLY
What is that?

JEFF
There's a little monkey on the roof.
(*We hear the monkey banging on the roof. It screeches.*)

KIMBERLY
Sounds mad.
(*The sound fades.*)

JEFF
There it goes, scrambled up that tree.

KIMBERLY
Look at it, though. It's staring at me. My mother had that face sometimes. Remember?

JEFF
Oh yeah. Look at that.
(*beat*)

Hey, there's a whole mess of them up there. Up in the branches?

KIMBERLY

Keep driving. They're kinda weird looking.
  (*hits Record again*)
Hey Carm, there's a bunch of monkeys here that look like Mom. I wish I had a camera.
  (*hits Stop*)
She's gonna like these, when she's old enough to understand them. You'll make sure she gets them, right?

JEFF

The tapes?

KIMBERLY

Because if I mail them, my Mom might just throw them out. I wanna make sure she gets them.

JEFF

She'll get them.

KIMBERLY

You'll make sure though, right?

JEFF

Yeah.

KIMBERLY

God, this place reeks. You smell that?

JEFF

There's a hippo in the road.

KIMBERLY

Look at that.
  (*presses Record*)
You won't believe this, little sister, we've got a hippo in front of us.

JEFF

  (*also into recorder*)
And it ain't moving.
  (*stops the car*)

KIMBERLY
Hey. We're not supposed to stop.

JEFF
What else can I do?

KIMBERLY
Go around it.

JEFF
There's a ravine.

KIMBERLY
The pamphlet says to keep rolling along, otherwise we hold up traffic.

JEFF
It's closing time. We were the last ones in.

KIMBERLY
Still, I don't want those monkeys coming back here.

JEFF
(into the recorder)
Kim's afraid of the monkeys.

KIMBERLY
We're just supposed to sit here?

JEFF
I can do an anagram.

KIMBERLY
No thanks.

(They sit in silence. After a couple beats, JEFF looks over at KIM. She looks over at him. They look away. An uncomfortable pause. They look at each other again, and eventually, after much tension, lean in and kiss.

They separate and sit in silence for a couple more beats, happy but petrified. KIM *notices the tape recorder, embarrassed.)*

KIMBERLY
I left the tape recorder on.

JEFF

Really?

KIMBERLY

We can save it for posterity.
   (*hits Stop*)

JEFF

Cool.
   (*pause*)
Where do you wanna go next?

KIMBERLY

Colonial Williamsburg.

JEFF

Very nice choice.

KIMBERLY

And then Busch Gardens. Sea World. Universal. We'll spend at least a week in Florida. We've got enough money for that, right?

JEFF

More than enough.

KIMBERLY

I hear they have nice dance clubs in Miami.

JEFF

Oh yeah?

KIMBERLY

Then we'll head West.

JEFF

The hippo's moving.

KIMBERLY

Grand Canyon, Mount Rushmore—
   (JEFF *turns the key in the ignition, but the engine just whirs without turning over.*)

KIMBERLY

What's the matter?
   (*He tries again, but the car won't start.*)

JEFF
Your Dad was right about this piece of junk car.

KIMBERLY
Where are those guys in the jeeps?

JEFF
I hope they didn't go home early.

KIMBERLY
Honk the horn.
(He does.)

JEFF
You see anyone?

KIMBERLY
No.
(He honks some more.)

KIMBERLY
All right, stop honking. You're pissing off that hippo.

JEFF
Screw him. If he hadn't stopped in the middle of the road—
(honks some more)

KIMBERLY
Now it's coming over here.
(JEFF *tries to start the car.)*

KIMBERLY
You see what you did?
(Faintly, we hear the sound of the monkey.)

KIMBERLY
And there's that monkey again.
(The sound of the monkey on the roof, only it's multiplied.)

JEFF
Sounds like more than one.

KIMBERLY
Why'd you have to honk?!
(*We hear a lion roar.*)

JEFF
What the hell is *that?!*

KIMBERLY
Start the car!

JEFF
This doesn't seem safe!
(*The car still won't start.*)

JEFF
It won't go!

KIMBERLY
Try it again!

JEFF
What kind of family entertainment *is* this?!

KIMBERLY
Stay calm!

(JEFF *tries to restart the car, but to no avail. The swirling animal shapes from the end of Act One return, the projections spinning around them as we hear various animals descending upon them, clawing at the car, roaring, screeching. The sound is overwhelming. It goes on for several beats, until—*

The engine finally turns over.)

JEFF
There she goes!

KIMBERLY
Go! Go!

(*And they pull away. The sounds fade, the spinning animals fade, and they are on their way.* KIMBERLY *looks behind her. They drive in silence for a couple of beats. Then they get sort of punch-drunk from the thrilling experience.*)

KIMBERLY
That was so weird.

JEFF
They still back there?

KIMBERLY
Just keep going.

JEFF
They running after us?

KIMBERLY
Turn here. That was insane.

JEFF
Are they gone?

KIMBERLY
Won't have that problem in Colonial Williamsburg.

JEFF
They gone, though?

KIMBERLY
Yeah, they're gone.

JEFF
You sure?

KIMBERLY
We're good. Relax.
   (*clicks on the radio*)
Just keep driving.
   (*The radio plays swing music as the lights slowly fade on the giddy teens.*)